_____

TO

_____

FROM

_____

OCCASION

The Jesus Code
© 2014 by O. S. Hawkins

All rights reserved. No portion of this book may be reproduced, stored in a retrieval system, or transmitted in any form or by any means—electronic, mechanical, photocopy, recording, scanning, or other—except for brief quotations in critical reviews or articles, without the prior written permission of the publisher.

Published in Nashville, Tennessee, by Thomas Nelson.

Cover design by Bruce DeRoos at Left Coast Design.

Thomas Nelson titles may be purchased in bulk for educational, business, fund-raising, or sales promotional use. For information, please e-mail SpecialMarkets@ThomasNelson.com.

Unless otherwise noted, Scripture quotations are taken from THE NEW KING JAMES VERSION®. © 1982 by Thomas Nelson, Inc. Used by permission. All rights reserved.

Scripture quotations marked KJV are taken from the KING JAMES VERSION.

Scripture quotations marked NASB are taken from the NEW AMERICAN STANDARD BIBLE®. © The Lockman Foundation 1960, 1962, 1963, 1968, 1971, 1972, 1973, 1975, 1977, 1995. Used by permission.

ISBN-13: 978-0-529-10082-5
ISBN-13: 978-1-4041-1076-2 (Custom)

Printed in China

18 19 20 21 22 DSC 5 4 3 2 1

www.thomasnelson.com

THE *Jesus* CODE

52 Scripture Questions Every Believer Should Answer

O. S. Hawkins

COUNTRYMAN®
A Division of Thomas Nelson Publishers

THOMAS NELSON®
Since 1798

NASHVILLE   MEXICO CITY   RIO DE JANEIRO

Dedication

To those special and sacrificial pastors, their wives, and in most cases, their widows in Mission:Dignity who have given their lives to serving others so often in "out of the way places," and who are now in their declining years. While in ministry they lived in church-owned homes and received smaller salaries, and now, in their retirement years, are in financial need. We are on a mission to bring them dignity, and it is an honor being Christ's hand extended to them. All royalties from The Jesus Code *and* The Joshua Code *go to support these sweet servants through Mission:Dignity.*

(Learn more about Mission:Dignity at www.guidestone.org/missiondignity)

TABLE *of* CONTENTS

INTRODUCTION

*R*ecently, while reading through the four Gospels—
Matthew, Mark, Luke, and John—I was captured by
something I had read a thousand times but had never really
seen: on page after page, I noticed the Lord asking questions.

Think about that. Our omnipotent (all-powerful) and
omniscient (all-knowing) Savior was always asking questions.
It mattered not whether He was one-on-one, in a small group,
or among a crowd. He was continually probing and question-
ing His listeners. I became so intrigued by this observation I
decided to count His questions. The Gospels alone record over
150 questions that escaped the lips of our Lord—and these are
just the ones written down for posterity. John informed us near
the end of his gospel that if everything Jesus said and did had
been recorded, all the books of the world could not contain it
(John 21:25).

The more I thought about this phenomenon, the more I
became convinced that this was a distinctive code, a "Jesus
code," for us to follow as we journey through God's written
truth. And one thing this code clearly reveals: it is okay to
ask questions. In fact, good leadership is more often characterized by the question mark than the period, exclamation
mark, or comma. Those who continue to grow in spirit and in

wisdom ask a lot of questions. We have reached a dangerous point in our spiritual journey when we feel that we have all the answers and we stop asking questions.

Among the hundreds of questions asked in the pages of the Bible are fifty-two (one for every week of the year) that every believer should be able to answer. *The Jesus Code* will guide you on a journey through Scripture by challenging you to study a question a week and then meditate on the answer until it is firmly fixed in your heart. The journey begins with the first question asked in the Bible, "Has God indeed said . . . ?" and continues with every question believers should desire to answer before they get to heaven.

So let me pose a personal question: Are you ready to begin looking at the fifty-two questions in *The Jesus Code*, questions with answers that impact not only today but eternity? After all, some answers for life just can't be found on Google! Let's turn the page and begin with the first question recorded in Scripture.

1   Has God Indeed Said . . . ?

—GENESIS 3:1

*W*e had a really good start. Life began in a perfect paradise. The climate was never too warm and never too cold. We had no aches or pains, heartache or worries. We lived in perfect peace and harmony in the midst of a perfect garden. And we had dominion over everything *except* the "tree of the knowledge of good and evil," which God had forbidden us to eat (Genesis 2:17). We were doing wonderfully well . . . *until* the devil slithered into our world and asked the first recorded question in Scripture. It was cleverly designed to cause us to doubt God, His word, and His heart: "Has God indeed said, 'You shall not eat of every tree of the garden'?" (3:1). That simple seed of doubt took root in our hearts. From that time on, we have wondered, "Has God indeed said?"

Satan entered the scene of life just three chapters into the Bible, and the last time we encounter him is three chapters from the end. And the damage he has caused is seen on every page in between. This cunning creature was smart enough to know that doubt is deadly. He did not try to force us to eat the forbidden fruit. He simply tossed a seed of doubt our way, and we took it from there: "Has God indeed said?"

This cosmic conflict has not changed through the millennia.

Satan is still very much at work causing us to doubt what God has said to us in His Word. Satan's tactic is a clever three-pronged strategy designed to lead us—just as he led Adam and Eve—to personal defeat and separation from God.

SATAN'S DECEIT BRINGS A SELFISH DESIRE

The plan was simple. The devil made a brief appearance in the garden, and all he did was ask a question: "Do you think God really meant that? Come on. Do you think you would really die if you took a bite of that single little fruit? Be realistic. God knows that if you did, you would become a god yourself; you would know both good and evil." And that is the last we hear from our enemy. He is gone. That is all he did. And that is all he had to do (Genesis 3:1–5).

Our minds are like a hotel. The manager can't keep people from coming into the lobby, but he can keep them from getting a room. It is the same with our thoughts. It is not a sin when an impure thought goes through our minds. The sin comes when we give it a room and let it settle down there.

And Satan's deceit brings to the surface our sinful, selfish desires as well as a lack of trust. It was true then, and it is true now: once doubt gets a room in your mind, Satan's battle is half won.

A SELFISH DESIRE BRINGS A SINFUL DECISION

Once doubt had its foot in the door, three things happened in rapid succession. Eve "saw that the tree was good for food . . . pleasant to the eyes, and a tree desirable to make one wise"

(Genesis 3:6). Next she took it . . . and ate. Then she gave her husband a piece, and he ate. Bam! Did things ever change! Adam and Eve were booted out of the garden, and they ran in an attempt to hide from God.

Once the seed of doubt took root, a downward digression followed. First, Eve *saw*: she "saw that the tree was good" (v. 6). Then she *coveted*: it was "desirable to make one wise" (v. 6). Then she *took*: "She took of its fruit and ate. She also gave to her husband . . . and he ate" (v. 6). And finally, they *hid*: "Adam and his wife hid themselves from the presence of the Lord God" (v. 8). The pattern had been revealed.

King David walked that same path. He *saw* a woman on a rooftop bathing. He *coveted* and sent men to find out more about her. He *took*: he brought her to his palace and slept with her. He *hid* . . . to the hideous extent of having her husband killed in battle in order to cover his actions. All of us walk this path when we allow doubt to have a room in our minds. We are no different from Eve or David. If we do not break the cycle, we also will see, covet, take, and then spend our lives looking over our shoulder to see if we will be found out. Why does this happen? Because a selfish desire that has been allowed to take root in our hearts brings a sinful decision.

A SINFUL DECISION BRINGS A SURE DEFEAT

Adam and Eve "knew that they were naked" (Genesis 3:7). Duh! But before that point, God had been so much the center of their devotion and attention, they had not realized it. Now, with sin in the picture, they were focused on themselves! So they covered themselves with fig leaves. God caught up with them, and the buck passing began. Adam blamed his sinful disobedience on Eve: "She gave me the fruit to eat." In fact, Adam even shared some of the blame with God: "You gave her to me." Eve said, "The devil made me do it!" Clearly, human nature hasn't changed much at all. Someone besides us is almost always to blame for all of our wrong decisions and all of our defeats.

But God, in His grace, intervened. Fig leaves would never suffice. So God took an innocent animal (a foreshadowing of the Lamb of God), killed it, and covered Adam and Eve with its skins. When that little animal took its last breath, it became the first to experience the deadly toll that sin takes. Strange, isn't it, that the whole scenario began with a simple question: "Has God indeed said?" It was designed to cause us to doubt God and His word, and that plan succeeded. Doubt is deadly.

And the bottom line? God placed man in a perfect paradise; Satan entered briefly and sowed a seed of doubt; we fell. God drove our first parents out of paradise, and you and I have been trying to get back home—back into God's presence—ever since. The Bible is the record of this heartbreaking journey in search of what we once enjoyed: the account begins in Genesis with paradise lost, and it ends in Revelation with paradise regained! Right now we are exiles from Eden. But God has made a way through Jesus Christ who, incidentally, is still asking, "Why did you doubt?" (Matthew 14:31).

Q & A: *"Has God indeed said . . . ?"* The answer is a resounding, "Yes, He certainly has." And what He says in His Word is true. We can trust Him. Remember this week that doubt is deadly when the Deceiver comes to you in various ways to get you to doubt what God has said in His Word.

2   SHALL NOT *the* JUDGE *of* ALL *the* EARTH DO RIGHT?

—GENESIS 18:25

*I*n my decades of Christian service, far and away the most often asked question has been something like this: "What about the person who has never even heard the name of Jesus? God will let them into heaven, won't He?" This is usually accompanied by such follow-up questions as, "What about those devout and sincerely religious persons of other faiths who spend a lifetime in service and worship?" and "What about our Jewish friends? Are they the 'other sheep' Jesus referred to as His own who are 'not of this fold' (John 10:16)?"

Abraham's "Shall not the Judge of all the earth do right?" (Genesis 18:25) is obviously a rhetorical question. He asked it not as much to gain information as to emphasize a point. A rhetorical question really expects no answer; it is already known. In this case, shall God, ultimately, "do right"? Absolutely! Rest assured of this. Even Job reminded us that our great God is "excellent in power, in judgment and abundant justice" (Job 37:23). David, the psalmist of Israel, added, "The judgments of the LORD are true and righteous altogether" (Psalm 19:9).

So who *is* the Judge going to allow into heaven? There are three theological persuasions when it comes to the issue of who is going to heaven. *Inclusivism* teaches that men and women are saved by general revelation and that, when all is said and done, no one will be left out; everyone is "included" in the atonement. *Pluralism* teaches that there is a plurality of ways one can get to heaven. The pluralist tells us that we are all going to the same place; different religions are simply getting there on different roads, but all faith claims are true and valid. *Exclusivism* teaches that faith in Christ and in Christ alone is the only way to the Father's house. Or, as Jesus Himself put it, "I am the way, the truth, and the life. No one comes to the Father except through Me" (John 14:6).

There are many issues hard to understand that must be left in the eternal councils of the Godhead. I will be the first to admit there is much we do not know, but there is also much we do know. What we do know from God's Word is the focus of this chapter. We'll look at two fatal flaws that are prevalent when dealing with the question at hand. Those who hold out the hope that heaven is open to those who simply have never heard is based on a *presumption* and an *assumption*.

FATAL FLAW #1: A PRESUMPTION

The presumption on the part of many proponents of inclusivism is that those who have never heard have some sort of special dispensation that will provide them a different way into eternal life.

But the same Bible that tells us God is a God of love also tells us He is a God of justice who must punish our sin. In a reading of Genesis, we find God's justice revealed several times before arriving at Genesis 18:25. God judged Cain for killing his brother Abel (Genesis 4). God judged the entire world with a great flood in the days of Noah (Genesis 7). At the Tower of Babel, God judged harshly man's self-reliance and sheer arrogance (Genesis 11). And who can ever forget what happened when the judgment of God fell on Sodom and Gomorrah (Genesis 19)? God's judgment is always true and always righteous.

Space does not permit us to hear out Paul on this matter. All one must do is read Romans 1–3 for a complete explanation of how we are all guilty before a righteous Judge. Those who have never heard the gospel are not condemned because they have neglected or rejected Christ. They, like all of us, are "condemned already" because creation speaks of Him (John 3:18, Romans 1:20) and because our own conscience testifies of Him as well (Romans 2:15–16).

If it were possible, however, that men and women could be saved simply by *not* hearing about Jesus and His plan of salvation, then there is something we, as believers, should get busy doing: we should shutter every church, recall every missionary, send every pastor/teacher to be a greeter at Walmart, and burn every Bible we can find. Then, in just a few short years, everyone would be on their way to heaven. Paul, however, said, "How shall they believe in Him of whom they have not heard? And how shall they hear without a preacher?" (Romans 10:14). There were two times in human history when the whole world knew of God's plan of redemption. Adam and Eve knew, and Noah, his wife, their sons, and their wives knew. Along the way we have failed to take the gospel to all people on the planet who don't yet know Jesus or God's plan of redemption. This is still our Great Commission from Christ.

FATAL FLAW #2: AN ASSUMPTION

The assumption on the part of many people is that there are those who are innocent and, as such, should be admitted into heaven. What about that man way up in the remote, untouched mountain regions of Nepal? Or that woman so far back in the African bush that no missionaries have ever passed her way? Do I believe that an innocent person can go to heaven without coming to Christ? Yes—but that person doesn't exist! There is no such thing as an innocent person. Paul taught, "There is none righteous, no, not one" (Romans 3:10). That includes me. That includes you. That includes the Bedouin nomad in a Middle Eastern goat-haired tent, the Buddhist burning incense in China, and the Hindu trying to appease God at the banks of the Ganges in India.

We are not condemned because we reject the claims of Christ. We are lost because we "all have sinned and fall short of the glory of God" (v. 23). Long before I ever had an opportunity to neglect or reject Christ, I was without hope. That's because I was born with an inherent sin nature passed down by my relatives, Adam and Eve. My own parents never had to teach me to disobey; that came naturally. My mom and dad had to teach me *to* obey.

So why did God permit His only Son to die on the cross? Love was His primary motive, but He was also demonstrating to us His justice. Sin cannot go unpunished. In His great love for us, He poured out His justice on Christ, who took our punishment and died in our place. He died my death in order that I may live His life. He took my sin so I could take on His righteousness. It is our response to this justice that determines our eternal destiny.

Interestingly, God did not put me on His Judgment Committee . . . nor did He assign me to the Election Committee. He put me on the Nominating Committee, and it so happens that many of those with whom I share the gospel and thereby nominate for salvation, He seems to accept into His forever family.

Q & A : *"Shall not the Judge of all the earth do right?"* Yes! Absolutely! Certain judgments may not look "right" to us, but this question calls for a heart check, a spiritual EKG on the part of each of us. After all, only God sees and knows what is really in the heart of man. That's why there will be many people in heaven some of us never thought would be there. And there will be some we thought would, but may not. It is because, when all is said and done, "the Judge of all the earth will do what is right!"

3   HOW THEN CAN I DO THIS GREAT WICKEDNESS, *and* SIN AGAINST GOD?

—GENESIS 39:9

*T*his question comes in the midst of a great moral inter-section in the life of Joseph. Few people enjoyed the measurable and meteoric success of Joseph. At seventeen, he was sold to travelers by his jealous brothers. He was taken by the Ishmaelites into Egypt and sold as a slave. Then, while faithfully serving in his master's house, his master's wife attempted to seduce him. When Joseph refused her advances, she falsely accused him of rape, an accusation that landed Joseph in an Egyptian prison. Then, through a series of miraculous events, he was released and, by the age of thirty, Joseph was ruling as, virtually, the prime minister of Egypt, the most progressive nation on earth. It is no wonder the Bible records, "The LORD was with Joseph, and he was a successful man" (Genesis 39:2).

Long before this series of events began to unfold, he had a dream that was recorded for us in Genesis 37. God revealed to Joseph that he would one day be the leader of a great nation and that others, including his own brothers, would bow down before him. Joseph never forgot this dream, this God-given vision. Along the way, however, Joseph would have to contend with three great enemies to success in life. One is *discouragement*: we have a dream about what God wants us to do, we encounter a few obstacles along the way, and discouragement keeps us from our potential. Another enemy to success is *diversion*: we have a dream, and something diverts us from pursuing and reaching that goal. In Joseph's case, it was false charges made by a beautiful older woman. If we overcome the first two, then *doubt* will find its way into our path: we have a dream, and in a time of testing, we too often give in to doubt. Joseph faced all three of these enemies.

WHEN TEMPTED BY DISCOURAGEMENT, FACE GOD-ALLOWED DIFFICULTIES

Joseph had a dream, a goal for his life, but nothing was going right as he pursued that dream. His brothers sold him out. He was hustled out of his country into a strange land and sold as a slave. What a contrast to being his father's favorite son, as he'd clearly been back home. And what reasons for discouragement!

People react to discouragement in various ways. Job *feared* his difficulties, saying, "The thing I greatly feared has come upon me" (Job 3:25). Elijah under the juniper tree *frowned* and prayed that he might die (1 Kings 19:4). The prodigal's elder brother in Luke 15 *fumed* when difficulty came: "He was angry and would not go in" to the party (v. 28). Moses *fussed* about his difficulties (Exodus 5:22–23), and Jonah tried to *flee* from them (Jonah 1:3).

In sharp contrast, Joseph *faced* his difficulties head on.

Whatever came his way, whether on the slave block, in his master's house, or in prison, whenever he was tempted to get discouraged—he faithfully continued to trust God's promises. When we are pursuing a dream, we aren't to fear or flee obstacles that come our way; we must face them.

WHEN TEMPTED BY DIVERSION, FLEE GODLESS DESIRES

Once Joseph overcame discouragement, diversion came knocking. The master's wife burned with lust and passion for this young Hebrew, and the timing seemed perfect for her to approach him. Think about it. The master was away from home. Nobody would know about the rendezvous. She certainly wouldn't tell! Most would have been flattered by the attention, but when this diversion arose, Joseph got out of there. He ran the opposite direction. He fled those godless desires of the heart. Hear him saying to her, "How then can I do this great wickedness, and sin against God?" Joseph knew that all sin is primarily against God; Joseph would not only be sinning against her husband.

Joseph was able to resist because he took a strong stand from the woman's very first advance (Genesis 39:8). Many people succumb to immoral diversion because they don't say no at the very first. They flirt with it for a while. Not Joseph. He fled. He didn't try and fight it. He didn't try and faith it. He fled. He ran.

Remember, God had given Joseph a dream, so Joseph was single-minded in his pursuit of that dream: nothing, not discouragement or diversion, would keep him from pursuing his dream.

WHEN TEMPTED BY DOUBT, FOLLOW GOD-GIVEN DREAMS

If Satan can't get you off track with discouragement or diversion, he will next try to get you to doubt that your dream came from God in the first place.

You may know the story well. Can you imagine what must have been going through Joseph's mind while sitting in that Egyptian jail cell when he had done nothing wrong?! He had been a loyal and faithful servant to his master, only to be rewarded with a false and trumped-up charge of attempted rape. Now he was in prison, and it seemed the guards had thrown away the key. Earlier God had told Joseph he'd be the leader of a great people, but that dream now seemed so very distant and its fulfillment so humanly impossible. Satan was bombarding Joseph with arrows of doubt: Had God really sent that dream? Or was it just some boyhood ambition?

God was testing Joseph. How do we know? David later recorded that God "sent a man before [the people]—Joseph—who was sold as a slave. They hurt his feet with fetters, he was laid in irons. Until the time that his word came to pass, the word of the LORD tested him" (Psalm 105:17–19). Could it be that when our own goals seem so far away and unreachable, God tests us to see if we are trusting in the living God or merely looking to Him to bless us?

So what did Joseph do? He simply kept following his God-given dream. He didn't say a word. He trusted in his God, in spite of doubtful circumstances.

Learn from Joseph. Make sure your dream is from God, then keep following it. Abraham heard God's voice and obeyed it. Joseph was led by his dream. We don't put our trust in audible voices or dreams today. Why? We have something they didn't have, the final and complete revelation of God to man: the Bible. We have a God who still speaks to us today, by His Spirit and through His Word.

Have a dream—and follow it. And when you are tempted to be discouraged, face your God-allowed difficulties. When you are tempted by diversion, flee those godless desires. And, again, when tempted to doubt, follow your God-given dream. When you do, and when that dream becomes reality, then what was said of Joseph just might be said of you: "The LORD was with him; and whatever he did, the LORD made it prosper" (Genesis 39:23).

Q & A: *"How then can I do this great wickedness, and sin against God?"* It would be a much better world if each of us asked ourselves this question when we arrive at our own temptation fork in the road, deciding which way to turn. The most tragic thing about our sin is that it is not simply against ourselves or someone else; when we sin, we sin against God. It is so serious that it necessitated Christ's death on the cross. Face those God-allowed difficulties, flee those godless diversions, and follow your God-given dream!

4   WHO AM I?

—EXODUS 3:11

*W*ho am I . . . ?" The stuttered question was spoken through dry lips.

It had been business as usual on the backside of the desert. Moses had been leading the nomadic life of a lonely shepherd for forty years now. This morning was no different from the thousands of others in his experience—or so he thought. Had the late Walter Cronkite been reporting this event we would have heard those oft repeated words, "And this has been a day like any other has been . . . except . . . you were there!"

Try to imagine Moses' absolute amazement as he witnessed a nondescript little bush on fire, yet not being consumed. Then the voice of God came from the bush and commanded Moses to return to Egypt, stand before Pharaoh, and demand the release of the Israelites from slavery. No small task! And Moses' immediate response was "Who me? Who am I? I can't speak well. You must have me confused with someone else!"

This is a completely opposite response to Isaiah's response to God's call which we will see later in chapter twenty-one. Isaiah said, "Here am I! Send me" (Isaiah 6:8). Listen to Moses as he responds to his call, saying: "Who am I to do that job? You need to send someone else!" Even though Moses had been educated in the finest private schools of the most progressive nation of the world, forty years of isolation had taken their toll on his self-confidence. Forty years alone will lead anyone to ask, "Who am I?" Yet *Who am I?* is an appropriate question for each of us to ask ourselves.

Moses epitomizes one who is suffering from a poor self-image and little self-confidence. Unfortunately, many believers today spend their lives posturing from a low self-image. Proverbs 23:7 reminds us that as a man "thinks in his heart, so is he." I am not so idealistic as to think that in reading this brief chapter a lifetime of low self-image can be translated into one that is healthy and positive. However, I am emboldened enough by my faith to believe that new thought patterns can begin to replace the lies and enable you to find your self-worth in your position in Christ. So who are you really? Let's find out.

AN EXPLANATION

Who am I? The Bible reveals that we are a composite of "spirit, soul, and body" (1 Thessalonians 5:23). However, note that we don't phrase it in this order. We generally say "body, soul, and spirit." This, subconsciously, is because we are so body conscious, and that painful awareness too often determines our evaluation of who we really are. After all, the body is visible. We pet it and pamper it. We tan it and tone it. We measure it and weigh it regularly. But one day it will go right back to the dust from which God created it.

We are not just bodies, though. Our soul is the seat of our

emotions. It is our feelings about ourselves that too often dictate our own self-worth, or lack thereof. Our spirit is that part of us that will live as long as God lives. It is our spirit that connects with God's Spirit—spirit bearing witness with Spirit that we are His children. So who am I? I am a spirit-soul . . . I am just living for a few short years in a body.

The marketplace is loaded with books and videos on self-image, and most of these deal only with the physical side of our being. They tell us how to dress for success. They have clever formulas for obtaining the upper hand in relationships. They focus on weight loss and other aspects of our physical appearance. Then there are those that focus on the soul, on the realm of emotions. These resources tell us things like how to win friends and how to keep hold of our emotions so that we can obtain influence and advantage over others.

But I am *not* my body, and I only *have* a soul. I *am* a spirit. Therefore, the Bible is the best self-help, self-awareness, self-image, self-confidence book ever written because it explains who I really am. Again, who am I? I am a spirit made in the very image of God.

AN ILLUSTRATION

Jesus illustrated this very point for us in Luke 16 with the story of a beggar and a rich man who both die. Lazarus, the beggar, died and was carried into "Abraham's bosom," the Hebrew representation of heaven (v. 22). His *body* was in the grave, but *he* was in the bosom of Abraham. Why? Because Lazarus was a spirit, not a body.

And the rich man? Jesus said he ended up in hell. So his body was in the grave, but his soul and spirit were still alive. He could still remember. He still had emotions. He was tormented. And he was troubled about his brothers' destiny. This rich man's five brothers did not know God, and now banished in hell, this rich man knew that an eternity of punishment for their sinfulness awaited them.

Our only means of truly knowing God is by our spirit. It is impossible to have a spiritual relationship with Him based on mere human knowledge. As Jesus said to the woman at a well, "God is Spirit, and those who worship Him must worship in spirit and truth" (John 4:24). Without a relationship of spirit to Spirit, you can never know God because "the natural man does not receive the things of the Spirit of God, for they are foolishness to him; nor can he know them, because they are spiritually discerned" (1 Corinthians 2:14).

So when you ask, "Who am I?" know that you are spirit. That is your real identity and the seat of your self-worth.

AN APPLICATION

Since we human beings are in essence spirit, we cannot depend on the physical for a proper self-image. The clothes we wear and how we look should not determine our self-worth. Neither should our emotions—the soul part of us—determine our self-worth. All the positive thinking and pumping ourselves up, all our taking hold of our emotions will never provide a healthy or accurate sense of worth. Each of us must discover for ourselves who we really are: a spirit being led by

God's own Spirit (Romans 8:14). Only in the Person of Christ in us will we find true self-worth.

Finally, back to Moses. This timid, stammering, reluctant Moses went away from that burning bush to become the great emancipator of God's people and the leader of a great nation. This same man who began by asking, "Who am I?" is last seen in Scripture on the Mount of Transfiguration amidst the glory of Jesus Himself.

Understanding who he was because of God's power and grace gave Moses confidence and strength for the task he was called to do. Similarly, when our spirit connects with the Holy Spirit, then we will have an accurate and healthy self-image, for "Christ in you [is] the hope of glory" (Colossians 1:27).

Q & A: *"Who am I?"* No one on the planet ever has or ever will have DNA exactly like yours, and you, in all your uniqueness, are indescribably valuable to God. So remember that you are a spirit . . . simply living in a body for a short time. And I am convinced that if we fed our spirit as much as we feed our bodies, we would realize who we really are, and a God-given positive and powerful self-image would be ours. "Christ in you [is] the hope of glory!" (Colossians 1:27).

5   WHY HAVE YOU BROUGHT US UP OUT *of* EGYPT *to* DIE *in the* WILDERNESS?

—NUMBERS 21:5

*H*ave you ever felt like you were on your own journey of wilderness wandering? . . .

Few people had seen the incredible miracles witnessed by the Israelites. They had been delivered from death on the night of that first Passover. They had been delivered from slavery when they passed through the Red Sea on dry ground. Even as they wandered in the wilderness because of their rebellion, they were being led by a miraculous cloud by day and a stunning pillar of fire at night. And, as if that were not enough, God was feeding His children each day with bread that fell from heaven.

But we all have a way of forgetting yesterday's blessings, especially when we become immersed in today's burdens. So Moses records that "the people [in the wilderness] became very discouraged" (Numbers 21:4). They took it out on Moses and even on God Himself, asking, "Why . . . Why . . . Why have you brought us up out of Egypt?"—then their frustration burst forth—"just to die here in this God-forsaken wilderness?"

Too often we find ourselves walking in their shoes. Life has been moving along pretty well, but we didn't appreciate how good we really had it. Then we suddenly find ourselves with no direction. We see problems mounting all around with no apparent way out, and we point our own finger at God and ask the same question: "Why have You brought us up out of Egypt to die in the wilderness?"

Discouragement can have a devastating and sometimes debilitating effect on our own life journey toward the promised land. Yet Moses recorded this story for all posterity to reveal that discouragement has its reasons and results, but it can also have its remedies. After all, in the New Testament, Paul reminded us that "all these things happened to [the children of Israel] as examples, and they were written for our admonition" (1 Corinthians 10:11). Since that is so, we have much to learn from this particular stop on their long wilderness wandering.

THERE IS A REASON FOR DISCOURAGEMENT

It's easy to forget not just where we have been but also where we are going. When this happens—when we only have eyes for the "now"—discouragement comes easily. Then the accumulated complexities swirling around us have their own way of demanding our immediate focus and fueling our discouragement. The Israelites' discouragement boiled down to the fact that they did not like two things: the way they were being led and the way they were being fed.

These chosen people of God complained, first, about the

way they were being *led*. They began to murmur against Moses, but the real object of their complaint was God Himself. After all, Moses was simply following God's lead and relaying God's instructions to the people. But they didn't like Moses' leadership—and they rebelled.

Their other subject of complaint was the way they were being *fed*: "Our soul loathes this worthless bread" (Numbers 21:5). The manna the people hated, however, was God's gracious gift of sustenance to these multiplied thousands of people who were without a food supply. The manna fell fresh every morning—a picture, we later learn, of the sustaining life we can have in Jesus Christ, the Bread of Life.

When discouragement comes, it has a dastardly way of diverting our focus from God and His blessings to the circumstances and situations around us. The Israelites' situation boiled down to the fact that they did not want God's Word through Moses to lead them, and they didn't want God to feed them!

THERE IS A RESULT OF DISCOURAGEMENT

Discouragement left to fester can have devastating results. Ask any one of these Jews in the wilderness. They learned that when we openly rebel against God's leadership and provision in our lives, He often disciplines us for our own benefit: "The Lord sent fiery serpents among the people, and they bit the people; and many of the people of Israel died" (Numbers 21:6). These consequences may seem overly harsh, to say the least. But there is a deeper lesson here for all of us. In the Bible, the serpent is a picture of Satan and sin, and the serpent still comes slithering up to us exactly as it did in the garden.

In this Numbers 21 incident, the serpents' bites were *terrible* and, in some cases, *terminal.* Moses described the serpents' bites as "fiery" (v. 6), and when they bit, apparently every nerve in their victim's body turned into a burning ember. The pain was undoubtedly excruciating, and the same can be all too true of the results of sin. I am amazed that some people have the idea that sin is enjoyable and harmless in the long run. It is not. Sin always has consequences, and those consequences are often painful in a myriad of ways. Simply put, "the way of the unfaithful is hard" (Proverbs 13:15).

These bites were not only terrible, but some were *terminal.* Moses reported that "many of the people of Israel died" (Numbers 21:6). God revealed here—as He does elsewhere in Scripture—that death is the ultimate end of sin and rebellion against Him. Paul was very direct: "The wages of sin is . . ."—what?—"death!" (Romans 6:23). James, who centuries later would be the leader of the Jerusalem church, went straight to the point as well: "Each one is tempted when he is drawn away by his own desires and enticed. Then, when desire has conceived, it gives birth to sin, and sin, when it is full-grown, brings forth death" (James 1:14–15).

THERE IS A REMEDY FOR DISCOURAGEMENT

The people of Israel learned their lesson and changed their minds in a hurry. They ran to Moses and said, "We have all sinned, for we have spoken against the LORD and against you;

pray to the LORD that He take away the serpents from us" (Numbers 21:7). Moses did pray . . . and in response God made what seemed a strange demand. Moses was to make a bronze serpent and place it high up on a pole. When the people looked upon that serpent, they would live.

This strange-sounding command was a *sure* remedy because it was God's remedy. Moses didn't say, "Here is *a* way to be cured." He revealed that this was *the only* way. This was also a *sufficient* remedy. It didn't matter where a person was bitten or how many times. God's remedy was sufficient for healing. And, finally, God's strange remedy was a *sustaining* remedy. It never failed. Everyone who looked at the bronze serpent lived.

Exactly what does this incident with the bronze serpent have to do with believers in the twenty-first century? First, remember that when the resurrected Christ spoke to the two men on the Emmaus Road, His intent was to, "beginning at Moses," explain "to them in all the Scriptures the things concerning Himself" (Luke 24:27). Yes, that healing serpent lifted above the people and bringing healing foreshadowed Jesus, and thus, we find our Lord right there in the middle of the wilderness.

Fifteen hundred years later, when Jesus spoke to Nicodemus of His crucifixion, He pointed back to this wilderness event: "As Moses lifted up the serpent in the wilderness, even so must the Son of Man be lifted up, that whoever believes in Him should not perish but have eternal life" (John 3:14–15). And so it was. Jesus was lifted high on a Roman cross so that all could see Him, and to this day, everyone who looks to Him for healing from their sin—for salvation—lives . . . and lives eternally.

How much clearer could the remedy be? The remedy God has provided for death due to our sin is *sure*: Christ is not *a* way; He is *the* way. The remedy is *sufficient*: no matter how much we have sinned or how little, He is *sufficient* to provide forgiveness and to save. Finally, God's remedy for sin is *sustaining*: no one has ever looked to our Lord to be saved and been turned away. Look to Jesus and live!

Q & A: *"Why have you brought us up out of Egypt to die in the wilderness?"* Are you discouraged today? Remember from whence you have come and where you are going. And look to Jesus. He has brought you out of your own Egypt to take you into His promised land. Look to Him . . . and live!

6

IF *the* LORD IS *with* US, WHY THEN HAS ALL THIS HAPPENED *to* US?

—JUDGES 6:13

*W*ho of us has not asked this question? And probably more than once!

Gideon was about to battle the Midianites against seemingly insurmountable odds. The angel appeared and said, "The LORD is with you, you mighty man of valor!" (Judges 6:12). To which Gideon immediately replied, "Really? If that's true, then why is all this happening to us?" In times of discouragement it is not unusual for some well-meaning "angel" to come along and say the same thing to us: "The Lord is with you." But you've just lost your job. Your husband left. Your wayward teenager is in trouble. You are sick and your body is wracked with pain. When any of that happens, we might not say it out loud, but we are prone to echo Gideon: "If the Lord is with me, why has all this happened to me?"

We don't have to look very far to find broken hearts, broken homes, or broken hopes. Bills can't be paid. Relationships are slipping away. Business is not going well. Single moms are trying to hold their families together. There are a lot of us asking Gideon's question today.

Centuries after Gideon's time the apostle Paul not only encountered the reality behind this question, but he answered it for us in his letter to the Corinthians. Listen to Paul's situation: "We were burdened beyond measure, above strength, so that we despaired even of life. Yes, we had the sentence of death in ourselves, that we should not trust in ourselves but in God . . . who delivered us . . . in whom we trust that He will still deliver us, you also helping together in prayer for us, that thanks may be given by many persons on our behalf" (2 Corinthians 1:8–11).

Discouragement that leads us to ask "Why?" is a modern-day plague. It has a paralyzing effect when we let it become our home and we settle into it. But once we acknowledge and face discouragement's cause, we can move out of that discouragement and move into Paul's answers to Gideon's age-old question.

A PARALYSIS

Discouragement can have a paralyzing effect on us as it leads us to say, "I give out. I give in. I give up!"

"*I give out.*" This was Paul's testimony. He related that "trouble" came his way and he was "burdened beyond measure" (2 Corinthians 1:8). He felt hemmed in. He was in a tight place, in a vise, under great pressure. We don't know the exact essence of the problem, but everything was closing in on him and he was about to give out. Discouragement—then as well as today—can have a paralyzing effect on us.

"*I give in.*" Paul's discouragement was turning into despair as—I believe—he was asking himself, "If the Lord is with me, why is all this happening to me?" It is just as well that Scripture veils the real issue at hand for him. That silence enables you and me to insert into the narrative our own point of discouragement. I have certainly been there, asking Gideon's question, seeing the paralyzing effect of discouragement, and being tempted to say, "I give out. . . . I give in."

"I give up!" Continuing his downward spiral, Paul confessed that he "despaired even of life" (v. 8). Who would have imagined this great apostle—who rallied the Romans by saying, "We are more than conquerors" (Romans 8:37)—would feel so overwhelmed and so deeply discouraged and despairing? Discouragement can leave the strongest of individuals unable to take one more step.

Having lived on the Florida Atlantic coast for a decade and a half, I became well acquainted with many professional lifeguards. When they spotted someone in trouble in the ocean, the guards swam out to them but did not immediately lay hold of them. Instead the guards would tread water just beyond arm's length. Why? The drowning swimmer's kicking and thrashing and struggling could well take them both down and under. But when the struggling swimmers neared the end of their strength—when, in essence, they said, "I give out . . . I give in . . . I give up;" when they realized they were unable to save themselves—then the rescue began, and they were pulled safely to shore.

Some of us find ourselves in similarly treacherous waters. We know we're going under, but we continue to kick and scream. We see the Lord an arm's length away. Why doesn't He do something? He may be waiting for you to come to the end of your self. He may be waiting for you to acknowledge that you are more in need of a rescue than you realized when you started reading this chapter.

AN ANALYSIS

A good medical doctor will do two things in analysis for treatment: look for a cause and then search for a cure.

Look for the *cause*. Why does God allow such a degree of discouragement that leads us to ask questions like Gideon's? Paul indicated it is often to break us down. Why? In order to build us up. Paul revealed that his discouragement actually happened in order that "we should not trust in ourselves but in God" (2 Corinthians 1:9).

Most of us have been there. Some little victory comes our way, and we begin taking some of the credit and trusting in ourselves. Our Bibles remain closed in the morning. Prayer is pushed aside in the busyness of the day. Then something happens that makes us realize once again that "we should not trust in ourselves" (v. 9) but in the Lord.

A few chapters later in this same letter, Paul framed this truth by saying, "I take pleasure in infirmities, in reproaches, in needs, in persecutions, in distresses, for Christ's sake. For when I am weak, then I am strong" (12:10).

Search for a *cure*. The cure is twofold: it is in hope and in help.

Paul said that his hope and trust were in Christ (2 Corinthians 1:10). And his help? "You also helping together in prayer for us" (v. 11). The English phrase "helping together" translates one compound Greek word meaning that we are in this together; we need each other. The word picture describes men and women working together under the same load and not against each other. Hope in Christ and help from others is the cure, enabling us to find our way out of the paralysis of discouragement.

"If the Lord is with us, why then has all this happened to us?" Paul began his response by stating, "We do not want you to be ignorant . . . of our trouble" (v. 8). Most of us are just the opposite, often a little too proud to let our guard down. So we live with no hope, with little help, and, sadly, all too often, with no healing. Your discouragement can be cured by . . . "God who raises the dead" (v. 9).

Remember, the most recurring phrase in all the Bible appearing on nearly every page is this: "And it came to pass." Discouraged? This too shall pass!

Q & A: *"If the Lord is with us, why then has all this happened to us?"* The ultimate answer is wrapped up in the mystery of God's sovereign, all-loving, and perfect will. He has numbered the hairs of our heads, and He sees the sparrow when it falls. How much more does He care for you who are tempted to give out, give in, or worse, give up? He is with you!

7 IS THERE STILL ANYONE ... THAT I MAY SHOW HIM KINDNESS?

—2 SAMUEL 9:1

*I*s there anyone in your sphere of relationships to whom you could show some kindness?

It was King David's greatest hour when he asked this question. At this point in his pilgrimage, there was no blemish on his character or integrity. In fulfillment of the longstanding prophecy, David was finally sitting on top of his world—he was on the throne of Israel. King Saul, his predecessor and nemesis, had been slain by the Philistines on the battlefield of Mount Gilboa. Tragically, Jonathan—Saul's son and David's best friend—was also killed alongside his father. David grieved and lamented over their deaths, but sometime later, overwhelmed by God's goodness to him, the new king asked, "Is there still anyone who is left of the house of Saul, that I may show him kindness for Jonathan's sake?" (2 Samuel 9:1).

That's when David heard of Jonathan's son named Mephibosheth. Poverty-stricken, unshaven, crippled since a childhood accident, and living in hiding at a place called Lodebar, this man was totally unaware that he was in a covenant relationship with the new king.

There is no clearer picture of integrity in action than in this personal drama. David, of whom the psalmist Asaph would later say, led his people with "the integrity of his heart, and . . . the skillfulness of his hand" (Psalm 78:72). David now acted on his longstanding promise to his beloved Jonathan. This story reveals that a person of integrity is not only one who remembers his promises but one who keeps them as well.

A PERSON OF INTEGRITY REMEMBERS HIS PROMISES

This friendship between David and Jonathan begins in 1 Samuel 20. David, the young shepherd boy, had burst from obscurity and slain the giant, Goliath. Immediately, this handsome young man became the rage of Jerusalem—and burning with jealousy, King Saul set out to bring him down. Jonathan, however, knew that the Lord was with David, and these friends entered into a covenant relationship, each promising to care for the other's descendants. Later, Jonathan died in battle and David was crowned king. In the aftermath, he learned about a forgotten son of Jonathan who was still living.

In his boyhood, Mephibosheth had lived in King Saul's palace and enjoyed all the king's provision. Upon hearing of the death of both Saul and Jonathan, all of the palace servants fled for their lives. As they fled, a nurse picked up young Mephibosheth and, in her haste to exit, dropped him and crushed his legs, and he became "lame in both his feet" (2 Samuel 9:13). Mephibosheth hid in a filthy refugee camp plagued by poverty. The years passed, and he assumed he was at least safe there. Poverty-stricken and forgotten, but safe.

Meanwhile, David remembered the promise he had made to Jonathan and began to take care of this unfinished business. After all, Jonathan had saved David from death, and now he was determined to find out if he could help anyone left in the house of Saul who might still be alive. A man of integrity, David remembered his promise to Jonathan.

Tragically, in our modern culture, broken promises seem more the norm than the exception. Promises made at wedding altars are often forgotten. Campaign promises on both sides of the political aisle—like "no new taxes" or "if you like your doctor, you can keep him"—are too often conveniently ignored. But David's example from centuries ago illustrates that a person of integrity remembers his promises.

A PERSON OF INTEGRITY KEEPS HIS PROMISES

It is, however, one thing to remember a promise and quite another to keep it. David did both.

King David sent for Mephibosheth—and can you imagine how this man felt when the royal chariots circled in a cloud of dust and stopped at his little shack in Lodebar? Undoubtedly his heart pounded as he grabbed his crutches and headed out his door to what he must have assumed was a certain death under the new regime. He probably thought he had been found and "wanted dead or alive."

Now picture Mephibosheth after he arrives at the palace and shuffles into the throne room of the king. He falls prostrate in fear before David. And then he can't believe the tender words he hears David speak: "Do not fear, for I will surely show you kindness for Jonathan your father's sake, and will restore to you all the land of Saul your grandfather; and you shall eat bread at my table continually . . . like one of the king's sons" (2 Samuel 9:7, 11). David did not simply remember his promise to Jonathan; he kept it.

Now try to imagine dinner at King David's table with all his sons in attendance. The room is ornate and elegant, graced with oriental rugs and high-back royal dining chairs. A linen tablecloth covers the table and drapes into the laps of the king and his sons seated around. There is handsome Absalom with his flowing black hair resting on his shoulders . . . and there sits Amnon, the clever and crafty one. Later they are joined by Solomon. And then comes the sound. It is the sound of shuffling feet accompanied by the *clump, clump, clump* of crutches. Mephibosheth is taking his place among all the king's sons at the king's table.

Continue to use your imagination for a moment. Suppose no one is looking, so you quickly climb under the table. What do you see? Legs! You follow them around . . . one pair of muscular legs after another. And then you see two crooked legs dangling, not quite reaching the floor. That is the exact view Mephibosheth had of himself during those years in exile: he was nothing more than a pair of useless legs.

Now climb out from under the table and take a seat near David's at the head of the table. What do you see? Note how the tablecloth falls into each son's lap, covering their legs. From the king's view, Mephibosheth looks just like all the others at the table. And this, friend, is the view the Lord Jesus has of each of His own children, of you and of me. Let me explain.

The reality is, I was once like Mephibosheth. I too was crippled by a fall. I too lived in exile, in spiritual poverty. Then the King's chariots came to my Lodebar, and I was arrested, but not to be imprisoned. I was arrested by God's forgiving and freeing love. The Holy Spirit who came to me took me to King Jesus. At first I was uncomfortable and wanted to go back to Lodebar where I felt at home. But then I heard the good news, the gospel. I heard the King say, "I want to make you My own child!" If you think Mephibosheth had a good deal, it pales next to the new covenant Jesus offers you and me! And the really good news is, there is a place for *each* of us at the King's table.

People of integrity remember their promises and keep them, whatever the cost. Perhaps you made a promise recently, or even long ago, that you need to remember . . . and keep.

Q & A : "*Is there anyone to whom I can show kindness?*" People we encounter at the office and in the grocery story, people we live with at home and worship with on Sundays, are in desperate need of kind words and deeds. Divine opportunities are all around you every day. Make a conscious effort today to show kindness to someone . . . not for "Jonathan's sake," but for Jesus' sake. Remember promises you have made . . . and do what you need to do to keep them.

8 WHY HAVE YOU DESPISED *the* COMMANDMENT *of the* LORD, *to* DO EVIL *in* HIS SIGHT?

—2 SAMUEL 12:9

*M*oral earthquakes, like real ones, often occur when we least expect them. Both are preceded by ruptured fault lines, located below the surface, where pressure builds up, tectonic plates shift, and mass destruction results. Certainly, this was true in the infamous moral earthquake of David and Bathsheba.

It all transpired so quickly. One evening, "in the spring of the year, at the time when kings go out to battle" (2 Samuel 11:1), the idle and irresponsible king got up from his bed and walked around on the roof of his palace. From there he spied a woman bathing below. This woman was very beautiful, and instead of looking away, he fastened his attention upon her. It was only a matter of time before he would take the leap from looking to lusting.

Ironically, at this moment in his life, David had reached the pinnacle of success. He was the undisputed king of Israel. He had driven out enemies who had plagued his people for years. He was not only a political success but a spiritual success as well. God referred to David as "a man after My own heart" (Acts 13:22).

It is difficult to believe that such a great man could descend from such heavenly heights to such devilish depths almost overnight. But he did. In the moment of David's greatest God-given triumph, the beautiful Bathsheba entered his life. And then came sin . . . and even greater sin. But in the aftermath of their adulterous affair and the murder of Bathsheba's husband, the king was fortunate enough to have a friend who held him accountable. Nathan appeared on the scene to share an apparently innocent story that ended with a powerful and penetrating question for the king: "Why have you despised the commandment of the LORD, to do evil in His sight?" (2 Samuel 12:9). We can learn much about our own vulnerability to sin from David's tragic experience with sin.

RECOGNIZE SIN'S COURSE

All human beings—all around the world and throughout all time—have one thing in common: "All have sinned and fall short of the glory of God" (Romans 3:23). We don't usually enjoy admitting it. Yet David is Exhibit A of sin's course.

Note the downward digression sin takes in David's case. First, he simply *saw* Bathsheba, and this is not sin. We can't help but see some things. Also, it is not a sin to have thoughts pass through our minds. The problem comes when we don't allow those thoughts to "pass through," but instead, grab them and let them take root in our minds. Next, David *coveted*. He began to think about her. He inquired as to who she was—and whose she was. He deliberately began to plot out the parameters and possibilities of his seduction. His was a premeditated plan that would result in greater sin. And that greater sin followed: David *took* her. He brought Bathsheba to his palace and committed adultery with her. And, as though he was not deep enough in sin, David tried to *hide* his adultery, even to the extent of allowing her faithful husband, Uriah, to be killed in battle.

It makes no difference whether it is David, or Adam and Eve, or you or me. The course of sin is the same. It begins when we see . . . then we covet . . . next we take . . . and finally we try to hide, hoping against hope we will not be found out.

REALIZE SIN'S CURSE

David was desperate that his sin not be discovered. He tried to hide his sin with treachery, then with lies, and ultimately with the death of Bathsheba's husband. This is the curse of sin: once we indulge, it has its own way of taking over. It begins to completely dominate our thinking and can begin to control our actions. We find ourselves constantly looking over our shoulder, wondering if we will be found out. One lie is necessary to cover another, and then another lie covers that one, and on and on it goes.

David actually thought he could sin and win. He thought he could get away with adultery, lies, and murder. But like anyone else who has gone down this road, he was wrong.

REVIEW SIN'S CONSEQUENCES

David learned that the pleasures of sin are only for a season

(Hebrews 11:25). Bathsheba conceived as a result of her encounter with David, but their little boy died as an infant. What had begun in pleasure ended in pain and loss in several forms. But this was just the beginning of the heartache David would know from his own offspring. His son Amnon raped Tamar, his own sister and David's daughter. Learning of the incest, Absalom—another of David's sons—killed Amnon. And, as though that were not enough, Absalom later led a revolt against his own father and, during the battle, was killed by some of David's men. Hear the grief in David's lament: "O my son Absalom—my son, my son Absalom—if only I had died in your place! O Absalom my son, my son!" (2 Samuel 18:33).

In a moment when we might anticipate the illicit pleasures of the flesh, we somehow deceive ourselves, thinking we can satisfy our desires outside God's will without suffering any consequences. If only we would preview the consequences of our sin that are sure to follow. Sin's momentary pleasures are never worth the pain sin brings.

REGARD SIN'S CONVICTION

Nathan helped David realize that he had done evil in God's eyes. David's eyes were opened and his heart was broken. Anyone who has ever read his prayer of repentance in Psalm 51 can see the broken heart of one who has experienced the terrible consequences of sin. When confronted with Nathan's question, "Why have you despised the commandment of the LORD, to do evil in His sight?" David accepted full responsibility for his wrongdoing. In genuine remorse and repentance,

David admitted to God, "Against You, You only, have I sinned" (Psalm 51:4). Then the humbled king beseeched his loving and forgiving Lord, pleading, "Create in me a clean heart, O God, and renew a steadfast spirit within me. . . . Restore to me the joy of Your salvation" (vv. 10, 12).

David stands as an example to all of us that, by God's grace, we can know cleansing and forgiveness for our sin.

Q & A: *"Why have you despised the commandment of the Lord, to do evil in His sight?"* Sin is always evil in God's sight, and there is bad news and good news here. The bad news? The sin you attempt to cover, God will uncover. Just ask David. And the good news? What you uncover, God will cover. As Solomon, another of David's sons, rightly observed, "He who covers his sins will not prosper, but whosoever confesses and forsakes them will have mercy" (Proverbs 28:13).

9   Ask! What Shall I Give You?

—1 KINGS 3:5

*S*olomon was about to be crowned king. This was no easy assignment for a young man not yet twenty years of age. Furthermore, he was following in the footsteps of his father, King David, one of the greatest leaders and motivators of men in human history. At this time of his life, Solomon was pure and virtually void of pride. He journeyed to Gibeon to worship and humbly seek God's help and direction. There God met him and asked the new king, "Ask! What shall I give you?" which is to say, "What do you want from Me?"

What do you want? Everyone wants something. Some want extra financial resources to pay off mounting debt. Others want a husband or a wife. Still others are in search of meaningful work and a clear purpose in life. Understandably, the Lord's question caused Solomon to stop and consider his priorities.

Everyone wants something. What you want may not be what you need, but what you want can be a very good indication of where your heart is. Incidentally, there is a greater tragedy than not getting what you want. It is wanting something, getting it, and then realizing it is not what you wanted after all! We can all tell stories of people we know whose lives were ruined because they got what (or who) they wanted, only to find out it was not what they really needed to fill their longing.

So what do you want? Solomon had the right answer. His priorities were in order. He didn't have to think long and hard about his answer. Right away he replied, "Give to Your servant an understanding heart to judge Your people, that I may discern between good and evil. For who is able to judge this great people of Yours?" (1 Kings 3:9). Solomon wanted three things: He wanted God to work *with* him, not with others. He wanted God to work *in* him, not around him. And he wanted God to work *through* him, not for him.

ASK GOD TO WORK *with* YOU

Solomon first requested that God work *with* him, not just with everyone else (1 Kings 3:4–9). Solomon knew that what he needed was to first deal with his own shortcomings and weaknesses, not someone else's.

I remember a frustrated husband once saying to me, "If my wife would just line up with Ephesians 5 and be more submissive to my leadership in the home, things would be better." I let him know the best chance of this happening was if he began to do what it also says in Ephesians 5 and love his wife "as Christ also loved the church and gave Himself for her" (v. 25).

For many of us, the problems we face are always someone else's fault. Wives blame their husbands, kids blame their parents, we blame God, we even blame the dog. Had the old spiritual already been written, Solomon would have been singing, "It's not my brother, not my sister, but it's me, O Lord, standing in the need of prayer."*

What do you want? Solomon said, "Lord, I want to be right with You. I want You to work with me first."

ASK GOD TO WORK *in* YOU

Solomon knew that what he needed most was internal, not external. He asked God to give him "an understanding heart" (1 Kings 3:9). Too often we try to change our world with external forces. We have become pretty adept at protests, petitions, picketing, and politicking. Somehow we think if we scream a bit louder and beat our Bibles a little harder, we can effect change, when what each one of us really needs is an internal change, a change of heart.

Solomon said, "God, I need something inside me that I do not have: I need wisdom." Solomon had the greatest education money could buy, but he recognized the difference between knowledge and wisdom. Knowledge is the accumulation of facts; wisdom is the ability to use those facts to make good decisions.

Don't we all need "an understanding heart"? Again, Solomon could have asked for anything, but he knew that what he needed most was for God to work in him. One of the dangers of all the Christian literature and devotional helps today is that some only hear what God has said to someone else. Solomon said, "Lord I know You have spoken to David, but above all I want an 'understanding heart' myself." After all, if we have a heart that can hear from God, what else would we ever need to live life well?

ASK GOD TO WORK *Through* YOU

Too often we want God to work *for* us, to bless us, instead of asking God to work *through* us to be a blessing to others. Solomon asked God to work through him.

God is asking you right now, "What do *you* want?" Are most of your requests of Him designed primarily to bless others or to benefit you? Solomon chose the best, and God went above and beyond. The Lord said, "I have done according to your words; see, I have given you a wise and understanding heart. . . . And I have also given you what you have not asked: both riches and honor, so that there shall not be anyone like you among the kings all your days" (1 Kings 3:12–13).

Unfortunately, there is a sad postscript. Often what weakens our focus on God is the very blessing He gives us. When your blessings become your god, you stop hearing from God. Solomon was blessed with great power and God-given wisdom, yet his focus began to change. That change came ever so slowly at first, but when he was an old man, he was the bitter author of the book of Ecclesiastes. There he wrote about the folly of learning, laughter, liquor, lust, luxury, and everything else that seems so important in life. And Solomon's ultimate and sober conclusion is this: "Vanity of vanities . . . all is vanity" (12:8). In the final chapter of Ecclesiastes, we hear from an old man whose heart can no longer hear from God. Listen to the hard-won wisdom of Solomon's words: "Remember now your Creator in the days of your youth. . . . Hear the conclusion of the whole matter: Fear God and keep His commandments, for this is man's all" (12:1, 13).

What do *you* want? The good news is when you choose the best, God will more than bless.

Q $\mathcal{E}$ A: *"Ask! What shall I give you?"* Remember that what you want may not be what you need. Make sure you want God to work *with* you and not just with others. Ask Him to work *in* you and not outside you. And may your request be for Him to work *through* you, not *for* you. What do YOU really want?

*"Standing in the Need of Prayer," author unknown.

10   HOW LONG WILL YOU FALTER BETWEEN TWO OPINIONS?

—1 KINGS 18:21

An amazing aspect of God's love for us is the fact that He gives us choices. We are not His puppets. God is not some master puppeteer pulling our strings so that we play out our lives on stage exactly as He wants. You are God's cherished creation, not a puppet. He loves you so much that He allows you to make choices in life. While most of these choices are small, some are so significant they have the potential to be life altering.

One of my favorite spots in the land of Israel is the Carmel mountain range. Standing on its summit you see the beautiful blue waters of the Mediterranean Sea to the west. Looking east you see a spectacular panorama stretching from the Galilean mountains to the village of Nazareth and on down to the valley of Armageddon. It was on a crystal clear morning, without a cloud in the sky, that Elijah stood on this very high place and called for Israel to make a choice. Israel was ruled by King Ahab who "did more to provoke the LORD God of Israel to anger than all the kings of Israel who were before him" (1 Kings 16:33). Ahab was not God's puppet; Ahab's strings were pulled by his wicked wife, Jezebel.

He had abandoned the worship of the true God in favor of the false god Baal.

Elijah called for a confrontation between God and Baal on Mount Carmel, and this turned out to be the original Super Bowl! Ahab brought 850 false prophets and gathered the people of Israel. Elijah, standing alone but confident before this multitude, knew that one faithful person plus God is always a majority. So Elijah challenged the people to make a choice: "How long will you falter between two opinions?" (1 Kings 18:21). The followers of Baal decided that both sides would build an altar, they would both offer sacrifices to their respective gods, and the God who answered by fire would be recognized as *the* true God.

You may know the story. Baal was tested first. The false prophets of Baal whooped and wailed for hours . . . and nothing happened. Then Elijah repaired the broken altar, prayed, and "the fire of the LORD fell and consumed the burnt sacrifice" (v. 38). When the people saw the fire from heaven, they began to loudly profess, "The LORD, He is God! The LORD, He is God!" (v. 39). Thus is recorded one of the great victories of the Bible.

The pages of Scripture are replete with challenge after challenge to make right choices in life. Moses said, "I call heaven and earth as witnesses today against you, that I have set before you life and death, blessing and cursing; therefore *choose life*, that both you and your descendants may live" (Deuteronomy 30:19, emphasis added). Among Joshua's last words to his people were these: "Choose for yourselves this day whom you will serve. . . . But as for me and my house, we will serve the LORD" (Joshua 24:15). Luke recorded this statement Jesus made about an important choice: "No servant can serve two masters; for either he will hate the one and love the other, or else he will be loyal to the one and despise the other" (Luke 16:13). And, in the last book of the Bible, our Lord rebuked those who were lukewarm, "neither cold nor hot" (Revelation 3:15).

As Elijah's question confronts us across the centuries, it reminds us that our lives are not so much determined *for* us as they are *by* us as we make wise or unwise decisions. "How long will you falter between two opinions?" Elijah asked (1 Kings 18:21). Indecision is deadly, so learn from Elijah four important points about making wise decisions.

WISE DECISIONS EMERGE FROM OUR CONSCIENCE

The people of Israel were faltering, wavering, tottering between two choices in life. They were on the fence. They couldn't decide whether to follow Baal or to wholeheartedly serve the God of Israel. They needed to make a choice.

So Elijah appealed to their conscience first of all. These people, like so many of us, knew better than to follow after false gods. They had such a rich history of seeing God at work on their behalf. Time after time He had delivered them from catastrophes and destruction even though they were so unworthy. Now the line was being drawn. The fence straddling could not continue. Elijah appealed to their conscience so they might realize God's faithfulness to them and act based on that fact.

WISE DECISIONS EMBRACE REASON

Elijah appealed to human reason, to good old common sense. After all, Baal was the fire god. If anyone could answer by fire, it would be him. But the hours passed . . . and Baal was nowhere to be found, and no fire fell on his altar.

When we find ourselves at a decision point and have "faltered" for too long without deciding, it's important not to let our self-justification for obtaining our agenda overrule our common-sense thinking—sensible logic and reason. The Holy Spirit will guide and sway our common sense if we will truly listen.

WISE DECISIONS EMPLOY GOD'S WORD

When decision time came, Elijah reminded God that he had "done all these things at Your word" (1 Kings 18:36). It was the Word of God that pointed the direction for him, so Elijah faced his foe with the *right message*: he began with a reminder of the covenant relationship with the living God and the Jewish people when he referred to the "LORD God of Abraham, Isaac, and Israel" (v. 36). Elijah also had the *right motive*: "Let it be known this day that You are God in Israel" (v. 36). The prophet's sole motive in defeating Baal was God's glory. And Elijah had the *right manner* in the way he went about it: "Let it be known . . . that I am Your servant" (v. 36). Elijah veered away from any personal applause that might have come his way.

When we consult God's Word, we learn that He will give us supernatural wisdom if we will only ask (James 1:5–8). We also learn that there is safety and wisdom in seeking counsel from godly, trusted friends, for the Bible says, "In the multitude of counselors there is safety" (Proverbs 11:14).

We make wise decisions in our lives when we employ God's Word in the decision-making process. He will never lead us to do anything contrary to His Word.

WISE DECISIONS EMBODY THE HEART

When the people watched Elijah rebuild the broken altar, their hearts were moved. The pieces of the altar were silent witnesses to the broken fellowship between a people and their God. When Elijah took those twelve stones and carefully made the altar, they were reminiscent of the twelve stones their forefathers had left at Gilgal to forever remind them of how God had parted the waters for them in days gone by.

Once you recognize the importance of your conscience—of exercising solid reason in decision making—and once you have employed God's Word, then follow your heart.

So God asked, "How long will you falter between two opinions?" Poet Robert Frost wrote "The Road Not Taken" about making such a decision:

> Two roads diverged in a yellow wood,
> And sorry I could not travel both
> And be one traveler, long I stood

And looked down one as far as I could
To where it bent in the undergrowth;
Then took the other. . . .
I shall be telling this with a sigh
Somewhere ages and ages hence:
Two roads diverged in a wood, and I—
I took the one less traveled by,
And that has made all the difference.

Q & A: "*How long will you falter between two opinions?*" Are you reading these words, realizing you are on the fence and you just can't bring yourself to make a decision? Choose God! He will not fail you or forsake you—He loves you and has a plan for your life. Decide to follow Him. And remember, not to decide . . . really is to decide!

11   WHAT ARE YOU DOING HERE?

—1 KINGS 19:9

*H*ave you ever found yourself in a place where you heard God ask you, "What are you doing here?" Elijah did. And he heard this question in the immediate aftermath of one of his most victorious mountaintop experiences. Even though he was among the mightiest of all God's men, Elijah was given to spiritual depression. He was living proof of the fallacy that only those who know failure get depressed.

Depression is real. Just ask anyone who has had depression come knocking unwelcome and uninvited at their door. Since we are made up of spirit, soul, and body, sometimes depression is due to physical issues like a chemical imbalance, and this should be treated by a medical doctor. There is also a psychological dimension to some types of depression, and these soul issues should be treated by trained counselors. Then, like Elijah and many others of us, there is a spiritual depression that may lead God to ask us, "What are you doing here?"

After Elijah's great victory defeating the false prophets on Carmel, we now see him on the run. With the wicked Queen Jezebel (she even sounds mean) wanting him killed, Elijah ran for miles to find refuge, first under a juniper tree in the desert and then in the hidden recesses of a cave. And Elijah's story is too often our own. Yet it reveals something about the sources, the symptoms, and the solutions to spiritual depression.

SOURCES OF SPIRITUAL DEPRESSION

The same man who faced down 850 false prophets and watched fire fall from heaven quickly forgot God's responsiveness, faithfulness, and power and fled from a wicked woman. And this kind of *forgetfulness* is a source of spiritual depression. In fact, one of the most dangerous times in the Christian life is right after a great spiritual victory. Elijah acted as if yesterday's victories would suffice for today's commitments. He took his eyes off his God and put them on his enemy, Jezebel. When crisis comes and Jezebel knocks on our door, we—like Elijah—are prone to forget God's power and blessing.

Another source of spiritual depression is *fear*. Elijah ran because he was afraid. Fear is not an action; fear is a reaction to circumstances around us. The same is true about faith: it too is a reaction, not to circumstances but to the Word of God. Just the day before, Elijah had not been afraid of 850 false prophets, but the next day he reacted in fear instead of faith.

Fatigue is yet another source of depression. Elijah had spent hours on Mount Carmel expending himself of physical and emotional energy. After God had made His presence known, Elijah traveled from Jezreel to Beersheba, a distance of one hundred miles! He was exhausted. Fatigue keeps us from thinking with clarity, with courage, and with faith.

In addition to being serious enemies of our own spiritual

and mental well-being, forgetfulness, fear, and fatigue are also some very real sources of spiritual depression.

SYMPTOMS OF SPIRITUAL DEPRESSION

Sources and symptoms are not at all the same thing, and we need to remember that. After all, we cause ourselves greater problems when we treat the symptoms rather than the sources of our difficulties. In other words, we too often ask, "What?" when we should be asking, "Why?"

One of the sure symptoms of spiritual depression is *detachment.* Isolation. Withdrawal. These are among the first symptoms of depression. When Elijah went into the wilderness and "sat down under a broom tree" (1 Kings 19:4), he removed himself from others. He detached himself from community. He left those who loved him most and who could have helped him most.

Too often, however, well-meaning people seek to help those in spiritual depression by treating this particular symptom of depression instead of its source. They say to those who become detached, "Get out of bed. Get up and get busy. Do something. Get around other people. Don't stay in your house all by yourself." Treating the symptom does nothing to address the source of the depression. Then the issue becomes even more complicated due to treating the symptom and not the source.

Despondency comes on the heels of detachment. Listen to Elijah: "It is enough! Now, Lord, take my life, for I am no better than my fathers!" (v. 4). Hopelessness. Despondency.

Elijah was losing his will to live. Fear and fatigue clouded his thinking. We do not overcome spiritual depression by merely thinking positive thoughts! We are not depressed because we are despondent; we are despondent because we are depressed! But again, despondency is a symptom of depression, not a source.

Detachment and despondency led to *deception,* to a self-deception fed by faulty thinking. Elijah moaned, "I alone am left" (v. 10)—but God quickly reminded him that seven thousand other people had not bowed to the world's false gods. But Elijah was deceived, resulting in another symptom: *defensiveness.* "I am all you have left," Elijah responded, so preoccupied with himself in his depression that he only had eyes for his problem. People battling depression tend to be self-consumed, and they can't help it. Detachment, despondency, deception, defensiveness—these are symptoms of depression, not sources.

SOLUTIONS TO SPIRITUAL DEPRESSION

Interestingly, the first step in overcoming spiritual depression is to address your *physical* needs. It is significant that Elijah immediately fell asleep. And the first thing the angel that awoke him said was, "Arise and eat" (1 Kings 19:5). Proper diet and healthy eating habits coupled with adequate sleep and exercise are some of the best ways to fight depression and get oneself on the road to healing.

There is also a *personal* solution. Elijah understood that it was not as much "I alone am left" as it was "I alone am responsible."

And at that point God asked, "What are you doing here?" (v. 9). Good question—and I have often wondered which word God emphasized when He spoke this question. Maybe He asked, "What are *you* doing here? You of all the people in the world, Elijah? You once had such courage! What are you doing here, in such a state of depression and doubt?" Or perhaps God said, "What are you *doing* here?" and Elijah responded, "Not doing anything, Lord. Nothing but feeling sorry for myself. I'm just not much use to anyone right now." Or God could have said, "What are you doing *here* under this tree? And what are you doing in this cave?" Have you ever been somewhere that you knew God didn't want you to be? Stop hiding. Face the foe: face your depression. The answer to the question "What are you doing here?" will be intensely personal.

Isn't it strange that we often have to get under a tree or in a cave before we can hear God speak to us? One lesson of the Christian life is that we seldom learn our spiritual lessons on mountaintops. Those lessons are most frequently learned in the valley experiences of life when God comes to us and asks, "What are you doing here?"

The last time we see Elijah in the Bible, he was on another mountaintop, specifically the Mount of Transfiguration with Christ. No longer running from the Jezebels of the world, Elijah had learned his lesson. He didn't find God in the "strong wind . . . an earthquake . . . [or] the fire," but in what Elijah called that "still small voice" (vv. 11–12). And that "still small voice" just might be whispering in your heart right now, "What are you doing here?"

Q & A: *"What are you doing here?"* None of us is immune to moments, or even bouts, of spiritual depression. When it's your turn, don't treat the symptoms; your depression will only get worse. Instead, treat the sources of the depression and rest in the fact that God has the solution. And His solution still comes to us in that "still small voice" spoken to our hearts.

12 WHERE DID IT FALL?

*T*his question came from the lips of the prophet Elisha at a critical moment. His school of the prophets had outgrown its facility, so in a great team effort, the students began to construct a new building alongside the Jordan River. As they were cutting down trees for lumber, one of the young men swung his ax with such force that the ax head flew off the handle and sank to the bottom of the river. Everyone then focused on recovering the lost ax head. In the midst of the confusion, Elisha appeared and asked a simple question: "Where did it fall?" The student "showed him the place" (2 Kings 6:6). Elisha then took a small tree and threw it in at the spot where the ax head had sunk. And Scripture says, Elisha "made the iron float" (v. 6). The ax head floated to the surface, the young man picked it up, and the work continued.

The ax head is the cutting edge of the tool. Metaphorically, the ax head is the dynamic power of the Holy Spirit within us that gives us the cutting edge in life. All the education in the world will never suffice for the cutting edge. All the natural ability and giftedness in the world will never match the cutting edge. This is because the cutting edge is the life of Christ made real in us through the Holy Spirit. But if we lose the cutting edge in life, how can we recover it? Today's amazing story shows us the way.

THE PROBLEM SIMPLIFIED

As one young man was swinging his ax, the ax head flew off, and the man cried out the news that he had lost it (2 Kings 6:5). The fact that he even acknowledged the problem is significant. Too many of us who lose our cutting edge are too proud to admit it. Instead, we compensate for the loss. We go off to seminars to learn how to swing the ax handle, we polish the handle until it shines, we motivate our fellow wood choppers with positive thinking, and we often come up with a clever little slogan. Then we go out and beat on the trees with our ax handles and come back as bruised as the trees themselves. But too often the sound of falling trees is absent. Why? Again, some of us have lost the cutting edge but are too proud to admit it.

One more important point. Note that this young man lost his cutting edge in the midst of keeping up a busy schedule for God. Ironically, this is one of the most common places our cutting edge is still being lost today—when we get too busy doing things for God. And we will never recover our cutting edge until we, like this young prophet-in-the-making, admit that we have lost it.

THE PROBLEM CLARIFIED

The young man cried out, "It was borrowed" (2 Kings 6:5). The ax wasn't his; it belonged to another. Similarly, this is the way it is with us. We don't possess the Holy Spirit; He possesses us.

No wonder there was desperation in this young man's voice. He prefaced his confession with, "Alas!" The fact that the ax did not belong to him made him more desperate to find it. May you and I be as desperate to walk with the Holy Spirit!

THE PROBLEM IDENTIFIED

When Elisha came upon the scene, his first words were the question, "Where did it fall?" (2 Kings 6:6). The young man "showed him the place" (v. 6). After all, the place to start looking for something is the place where we last had it!

If you are among those who may have lost the cutting edge in life, the first step to getting it back is to admit it. You must then go back to the place where you lost it. Did you lose your cutting edge when your busy schedule squeezed out your morning quiet time? Or when the Bible you once opened each night remained closed on your nightstand? Perhaps you lost your cutting edge when you judged another or when bitterness took root in your heart. Or maybe you lost that ax head in the waters of worldliness or the pools of pride. The place to recover the cutting edge is to go back to the place where you last had it.

THE PROBLEM NULLIFIED

When Elisha saw the spot where the ax head was lost, "he cut off a stick, and threw it in there; and he made the iron float" (2 Kings 6:6). This man of God was willing to receive God's supernatural power. Are we? After all, iron does not float. Go to the physics department of your local college or university and the professor will explain to you the composition of iron, the composition of water, and why iron cannot float. In fact, floating iron is a scientific impossibility. And if the professor stops with that statement, he or she apparently doesn't know about the tree on which our Savior died, our Savior who can still make iron float today.

The supernatural power of God—will we receive it? We hear all around us today, "You can't heal that broken heart," and that's the same as saying, "Iron doesn't float." "You can't restore that broken home" is the same as saying, "Iron doesn't float." "You can't recover those broken dreams" is yet another variation of "Iron doesn't float"—and the list goes on and on. The stick—that little part of a tree—that Elisha threw into those waters, bringing about that miracle, was a foreshadowing of the tree on which Jesus won our victory, and it was a victory not just over sin but over life's hard circumstances as well. After all, our problems lose their hold on us when we believe that God still makes the impossible possible.

THE PROBLEM RECTIFIED

After Elisha threw the stick into the water, the young man had something to do. Elisha said, "'Pick it up for yourself.' So [the young man] reached out his hand and took it" (2 Kings 6:7). Again, it is not enough to simply acknowledge that we have lost the cutting edge, to admit that the power belongs to another, to go back to the place where we last had that power, and to receive the supernatural power of God *if* we ourselves don't—in an act of faith—reach out and take it back. The outcome of the whole story hinged on whether this young man would reach out and take the ax head. The outcome of your story hinges on whether you will reach out and take the Source of your strength and power. The young man did. Will you?

Once when Jesus was walking through a large crowd of people who were pressing in all around Him, He stopped, looked around, and asked, "Who touched me?" A woman in the crowd desperately needed healing, so she had simply reached out and touched the hem of His garment . . . and was made whole (Luke 8:43–48). Will you receive Jesus' power today by reaching out and touching Him?

Q $\mathcal{E}$ A: *"Where did it fall?"* The ax head is the cutting edge—it's the dynamic life of the Holy Spirit in a believer like you. Don't be content to swing just an ax handle at the trees in your path. Go back where you lost your edge . . . and pick it up. You'll be glad you did because there is a world of difference in something done *for* God and something done *by* God! The supernatural power of God is there for you: reach out and take it.

13   WHY ARE WE SITTING HERE UNTIL WE DIE?

—2 KINGS 7:3

*F*our lepers were sitting at the city gate of Samaria asking one another this question. And the fact that they were sitting got me thinking about how much sitting we Christians do. When we attend church services, we sit. When we go to mission committee meetings or Bible studies, we sit. When we rush to committee meetings, we sit once we get there. When we attend seminars, we sit. In fact, it seems most Christians spend the majority of their Christian activity sitting.

There are two senses that should characterize every believer: common sense and uncommon sense. We need both to be effective in the Christian life. But some of us only exhibit uncommon sense, or faith. By that I mean that some can become so otherworldly that they no longer connect with reality. This perversion of faith keeps us less involved in the world and ultimately confuses true faith with wishful thinking. Then, there are people who only use common sense. We become so practical in our approach to life and ministry that there is little spiritual and mostly logical, worldly dynamic to what we do. We explain away most of our life experiences in human terms. But God expects us to use both our uncommon sense—"without faith it is impossible to please Him" (Hebrews 11:6)—as well as good old common sense.

In 2 Kings 7 common sense takes center stage. The city of Samaria had been besieged by the Syrian army. Ben-Hadad, one of the cruelest generals to ever march an army, had the city surrounded for months. He had cut off all supplies, and the people inside the city were starving to death and living in fear. Outside the city there was plenty, but inside there was poverty. Outside there was determination, but inside there was desperation. And against this backdrop, we find the four lepers sitting at the city gate, not really inside but not exactly outside either. They weren't making the situation worse, but neither were they making it better. They were just sitting.

Finally, one of the four said, "This is crazy. If we sit here, we're going to die. If we go into the city, we will die. If we go out to the Syrian camp, they'll probably kill us. What do we have to lose?" So they set out, walking in the darkness, expecting to be ambushed at any moment. But nothing happened. They encountered nothing but total quiet. They entered the camp, and it was deserted. Why? God had caused the Syrians to hear what sounded like advancing armies, and they had fled in panic and haste. The lepers opened a tent and found dinner still on the table. Rushing in, they ate until they could eat no more. Finally, common sense kicked in again: "We aren't doing what is right. If we wait until the sun comes up, we'll be in danger. So let's go back now and tell the king of Samaria and our people." The four men returned and spread the good news, and the city of Samaria was saved.

There is a lot we can learn today from this incredible common-sense story from long ago.

COMMON SENSE SAYS IT'S TIME TO BE REALISTIC

No one knows how long these lepers had been sitting at the gate, watching the enemy lay siege on the city from the outside and listening to the cries of death from the inside. But one day common sense kicked in, and the four men faced reality. They said to one another, "Why are we sitting here until we die?" When there is no hope in the future, there is no power in the present. Finally they acknowledged and admitted to one another their dilemma.

What do people do when they realize hope is almost gone? Out of desperation, they use their common sense and do something. Are you sitting by your own gate, not really outside but not inside either? Common sense says it's time to be realistic about your situation and your options.

COMMON SENSE SAYS IT'S TIME TO BE RISKY

These four lepers had nothing to lose, so they took a risk. Listen in on their reasoning: "If we say, 'We will enter the city,' the famine is in the city, and we shall die there. And if we sit here, we die also. Now therefore, come, let us surrender to the army of the Syrians. If they keep us alive, we shall live, and if they kill us, we shall only die" (2 Kings 7:4). Common sense was whispering in their ears, "It's time to take a risk." Note the four *ifs* in this verse. Clearly, the four men had absolutely nothing to lose, so they took a risk, and the reward was greater than they had ever dreamed. The army they'd expected to see had fled, and the city of Samaria was now safe and free!

God wants His people to be a risk-taking people. Don't be numbered among those who spend their time justifying to themselves why others can do something and excusing why they themselves can't. Instead, remember the young girl who risked believing the angel's message that she was pregnant with the Messiah. Her husband-to-be also heard a message from an angel and risked becoming the brunt of every barroom joke in Nazareth to believe it and obey it. And what about those fishermen in Galilee who left their nets and risked their reputations, livelihoods, and families in order to follow Jesus of Nazareth? Even our Lord risked the cross because He believed that the Father would raise Him from death to life on the third day. Common sense can tell us it is not just time to be realistic but risky as well.

COMMON SENSE SAYS IT'S TIME TO BE RIGHT

These four starving men entered the Syrian army's abandoned camp and feasted on the food left on the tables of the soldiers who had fled into the darkness. But once again common sense kicked in, and they said one to another, "We are not doing right. This is a day of good news, and we remain silent. If we wait until the morning light, some punishment will come upon us. Now therefore, come, let us go and tell the king's household" (2 Kings 7:9).

Back within the city walls, the people of Samaria were

paralyzed with fear—the fear of a nonexistent army! Still, they were paralyzed in ignorance, cowering in despair, and totally unaware that deliverance was already theirs. Common sense won the day because it is never wrong to do right. Thus the *sitters* who became the *getters* now became the *goers,* and they returned home with good news that meant liberation from the Syrians. And the city of Samaria was saved. Common sense is still on center stage today reminding us when it is time to be realistic, when it is time to take a risk, and above all, when it is time to do what is right.

Q & A : *"Why are we sitting here until we die?"* It may be that you are watching the disintegration of your own hopes and dreams. Perhaps life that once promised so much has delivered so little. And there you sit . . . You aren't exactly outside the camp, but you aren't really inside either. In those situations, uncommon sense—faith in God—is important. Without faith you cannot please God. But common sense is important too. Is it time to be realistic? Is it time to take a risk? It is always time to do what is right . . . and it's never wrong to do right!

14   SHOULD SUCH *a* MAN *as* I FLEE?

*I*t's not just how we start a race that matters. How we finish is what's most important.

Nehemiah was not a prophet or a preacher. He was a layman, a civil servant, burdened with the reproach of Jerusalem's broken-down walls and burned gates. He was granted permission to return from Babylonian exile to be the rebuilder of Jerusalem. He assembled a competent and committed team, cast a vision, and managed the huge task. After a long six weeks of hard work, the completion was in sight. But before we read that "the wall was finished" (Nehemiah 6:15), Nehemiah came to a crossroads and was tempted to abandon the entire project in the last moment. He asked, "Should such a man as I flee?" (v. 11). He speaks to us, so many centuries later, of the importance of "finishing strong" in our own God-given assignments of life.

The last lap in any race—literal or metaphorical—is often the most challenging. All of us can recall people who quit even when the finish line was in sight. Nehemiah's enemies come on the scene in chapter 6 with one final, last-ditch effort to discourage his strong finish. Yet Nehemiah asked two questions that helped fuel his successful finish. When he was tempted to get off on side streets, he kept focused: "Why should the work cease while I leave it and go down to you?" (v. 3). And when tempted to get on the sidelines, he kept faithful and asked, "Should such a man as I flee?" (v. 11). It is not how long our race may be, nor even how difficult the task, but how we finish that is most important.

Nehemiah's goal was finally in sight. The walls were rebuilt, and all that remained was hanging the gates. He was on the last lap of a long race that had carried him over many hills and through many valleys. As he sprinted to the finish line, he shouted to us. Can you hear him? "Stay off the side streets! Keep focused!" and "Stay off the sidelines! Keep faithful!" Finishing our own task is a hallmark of success in life.

STAY OFF THE SIDE STREETS! KEEP FOCUSED!

Sanballat—Nehemiah's longtime nemesis—and his deceitful friends made a final attempt to derail him. They sought to trick him into a meeting that was designed to get him off on a side street. "Come, let us meet . . . in the plain of Ono" (Nehemia 6:2) was their invitation. Fortunately, a focused Nehemiah said no: "I am doing a great work, so that I cannot come down" (v. 3).

So often, when our own task is almost done, some Sanballat comes along, seemingly harmless, to get us to lose focus. What is Ono? It is nothing more than a side street. We have all gotten off on them at one time or another. I often did that literally during the fifteen years my family and I lived in Fort Lauderdale. It is called the "Venice of America" because there are more than two hundred miles of waterways within its city limits. There are thousands of homes on the canals that wind their way through the city, so water taxis are a popular mode of transportation. Those who live there and drive cars learn quickly that if you want to get anywhere, you stay on the main roads. Each time I tried to beat the traffic by taking a side street, I would end up on a cul-de-sac, a circle, or worse, a dead end into a canal. Ono may appear to be a good thing, but in this case the good is the enemy of the best.

So what can keep us off the side streets when we are so near a finish line? Focus—and Nehemiah had a laser-like focus: "I am doing a great work, so that I cannot come down. Why should the work cease while I leave it and go down to you?" (v. 3). Stay off the side streets! Keep focused!

STAY OFF THE SIDELINES! KEEP FAITHFUL!

No one who has ever played on an athletic team likes to be on the sidelines. No one who has ever aspired to be on stage takes joy in being in the wings. Nehemiah wanted to avoid the sidelines as well. Just before he completed his assignment, his adversaries made a last-ditch effort to derail him: "Let us meet together in the house of God, within the temple . . . for they are coming to kill you" (Nehemiah 6:10). Nehemiah knew that, as a layman, he was not permitted to go "within the temple." He hadn't gone down a side street, and he was not about to be put on the sidelines now. Once again, he responded with a question, "Should such a man as I flee?" (v. 11).

In contrast to Nehemiah's perseverance, we live in a day when we see a lot of men and women fleeing, running out on responsibilities and opportunities and away from risks. This escapism takes all kinds of forms. Too many wish with the psalmist, "Oh, that I had wings like a dove! I would fly away and be at rest" (Psalm 55:6). Guess what? You don't have any wings! You can't just fly off. You can't run out every time things don't seem to go your way.

Those who win in life finish strong. Life is like a golf tournament in that regard. Who most often wins the tournament? The player who plays the final few holes with intensity and passion. Even though the tournament consists of seventy-two holes, the last few quite often determine the winner. Who generally wins college basketball's Final Four? The team that plays strongest in the last two minutes. In the Olympics, the mile run is a high-impact event. The runner who finishes strongest in the last fifty yards is always the winner. In the courtroom, who usually comes out victorious? The opening arguments are important. Effective examination and cross-examination of witnesses are imperative. But it is the final argument that leaves the lasting impression on the jury.

No one ever finished stronger than the Lord Jesus. When the finish line for His race was in sight, He said, "I have finished the work which You have given Me to do" (John 17:4). The enemy tried its best to get Him on the sidelines. The crowd jeered, mocked, screamed, and spat. "If You are the Son of God," they shouted, "come down from the cross" (Matthew 27:40). But Jesus kept focused and faithful. And in the end He solemnly proclaimed victory: "It is finished!" (John 19:30). And, to prove it, three days later He arose from the grave.

Q $\&$ A: *"Should such a man as I flee?"* Of course not! Finish strong! Maybe you have fallen down on the track or hit the ball out of bounds. Get up and finish the race. Get back in the game. It is all about how you finish! Stay off the side streets. Keep focused. Stay off the sidelines. Keep faithful. Our Lord is standing at the finish line with His arms outstretched. Keep running toward Him!

15 IF *a* MAN DIES, SHALL HE LIVE AGAIN?

—JOB 14:14

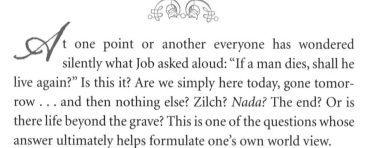

At one point or another everyone has wondered silently what Job asked aloud: "If a man dies, shall he live again?" Is this it? Are we simply here today, gone tomorrow . . . and then nothing else? Zilch? *Nada?* The end? Or is there life beyond the grave? This is one of the questions whose answer ultimately helps formulate one's own world view.

God has instilled within the human heart a longing for life beyond this earthly existence. Even paintings found on the cavern walls of ancient cave dwellers have depicted their desire to live again beyond this life. In Egypt, the pharaohs were buried deep within their great pyramids accompanied with weapons, eating utensils, even servants—evidence of their belief that there was life beyond this brief existence. The Native Americans of the Great Plains believed they would live again in the "happy hunting grounds." Clearly, God has supernaturally implanted within the human spirit a longing for life beyond the grave.

This hope for life beyond the present one has given rise to such beliefs as reincarnation within Eastern Religions. Various nuances of reincarnation are becoming popular in the West as well. It's an idea that exalts man and his own achievements. The premise is that man is sufficient to achieve his own perfection in and of himself. It may take him a few lifetimes to do so, but he will eventually succeed. Then there is karma. Its popularity is quite simple. If one does well in life, it proves one's worth. But should calamity come, it can be blamed on a past life. This belief is popular because little personal responsibility is involved. Hoping to live again in another physical life here on earth means living without any real fear of death, much less of judgment or eternal punishment.

Also fueling today's interest in life after death are accounts of near-death experiences. Every few years another bestselling book releases, describing someone's "death" and what that person experienced before returning to their body. Volumes like *90 Minutes in Heaven*, *Embraced by the Light*, and *Heaven Is for Real* have sold millions of copies. Clearly, Job's question sells today.

"If a man dies, shall he live again?" Job responded with an emphatic "Yes!" in Job 19:25–27. Hear his confident proclamation:

> For I know that my Redeemer lives,
> And He shall stand at last on the earth;
> And after my skin is destroyed, this I know,
> That in my flesh I shall see God,
> Whom I shall see for myself,
> And my eyes shall behold, and not another.
> How my heart yearns within me!

These words come from the lips of a man who had just lost his job, his health, his wealth, his friends, and most of his family. Yet his answer to his original question—"If a man dies, will he live again?"—is positive, pointed, and personal.

WILL WE LIVE AGAIN? THE ANSWER IS POSITIVE

Job said, "I know that my Redeemer lives" (Job 19:25). Job did not say, "I think . . ." or, "I hope . . ." Nor did he say, "I wish . . ." Job is rock-solid certain; he is absolutely positive that he will live again. There are no "ifs" or "buts" about it.

Is there life after death? God wants us to know with certainty that another life will follow our earthly existence and that it will be more than a million times a million times longer than this one. A thousand years from today we will be alive.

The apostle John put it like this: "These things I have written to you who believe in the name of the Son of God, that you may know that you have eternal life" (1 John 5:13). The Bible you often hold in your hands was written to you in order that you would be positive and have certain assurance, not only that there is another life after your time on earth, but that you can spend it with Jesus.

WILL WE LIVE AGAIN? THE ANSWER IS POINTED

Job indicated it was his Redeemer who is alive, and he would see Him after the destruction of his earthly body (Job 19:25, 27). This role of Redeemer is well illustrated in the biblical account of Boaz and Ruth (Ruth 4:1–4). Boaz, the kinsman-redeemer, foreshadows our own Redeemer, the Lord Jesus Christ. In order to fulfill the duties of a kinsman-redeemer, one not only had to be a member of the family, but had to be able and willing to pay a price of redemption. This is the essence of Job's declaration. His Redeemer would buy back his lost heritage. We too lost our heritage . . . back in Eden's garden. Our Redeemer has bought us back with the price of His own blood.

So Job said, "I have lost everything. So what if death comes? I know that my Redeemer lives and that in the end He will restore me. He lives, and I will live again also."

In Jerusalem today there is a beautiful garden and in it lies a famous tomb, but there are many famous tombs in the world. I have seen the pyramids of Egypt, famous for the pharaohs who lie inside. The Cave of Machpelah in Hebron is famous for holding the remains of Abraham, Isaac, and Jacob. In London, Westminster Abbey contains the bodies of Browning, Tennyson, Livingston, and other great Englishmen. In Mecca is the tomb of Mohammed, the prophet of Islam. All those tombs are famous for who is inside them. But the Garden Tomb, just outside the city walls of Jerusalem, is famous for whom it *doesn't* contain! Job's answer to life's question is pointed: "I know that my Redeemer lives!"

WILL WE LIVE AGAIN? THE ANSWER IS PERSONAL

Finally, Job emphasized that it is "*my* Redeemer" who lives (Job 19:25, emphasis added). Are you able to embrace that little two-letter word *my*? When Jesus, in His resurrected body, appeared before the disciples in the Upper Room, Thomas was present, and had already earned the nickname that sticks to him like glue—even today: Doubting Thomas. He had not been with his fellow disciples when the risen Lord first appeared, and he expressed his unbelief at such a miracle. But now, in the Lord's presence, Thomas no longer doubted. He fell before his risen Lord and simply exclaimed, "My Lord and my God!" (John 20:28). Is Jesus that personal, that real, to you? Can you say, "I know that *my* Redeemer lives"? If so, like Job, you are well on your way to answering the question of life after death.

In the midst of his great difficulties, Job's source of delight was seeing God in the next life. He knew that "in the end" heaven is a wonderful place. We will never see a hospital: there will be no sickness. We will see no funeral homes: there will be no more death. We will see no more counseling centers: there will be no more depression, heartache, or mental illness. Whatever takes the joy out of life will be gone forever for those who can say, "I know that my Redeemer lives!"

Q & A: *"If a man dies, shall he live again?"* Yes . . . somewhere! And those who have placed their hope in Christ, their Redeemer, will live with Him in heaven forever. For the believer, death is not about leaving home. It's about going home!

16

IF *the* FOUNDATIONS ARE DESTROYED, WHAT CAN *the* RIGHTEOUS DO?

—PSALM 11:3

A news reporter once asked someone, "What are the two greatest problems facing America?" The man replied, "I really don't know—and I really don't care!" And there you have it, the two greatest problems facing our nation: ignorance ("I don't know") and apathy ("I don't care"). No two single factors are working harder to destroy the very foundation of our nation than ignorance and apathy.

Three thousand years ago King David asked this very penetrating and probing question that's all too relevant today: "If the foundations are destroyed, what can the righteous do?" (Psalm 11:3). We are living in a time when many of the moral and ethical values that once formed the infrastructure of our great nation are crumbling before our very eyes.

George Washington entered the office of the presidency with these wise words: "The propitious smiles of Heaven can never be expected on a nation that disregards the eternal rules of order and right which Heaven itself has ordained." In 1796 he left office with this farewell: "Of all the dispositions and habits which lead to political prosperity, religion and morality are indispensable supports. In vain would that man claim the tribute of patriotism who should labor to subvert these great pillars." Sadly, our first president would not recognize his nation today. We can no longer pray at high school graduations, Christmas carols are forbidden in elementary schools, and long-held religious liberties are diminishing with each passing day.

What are these pillars that have helped America be a shining city on a hill before the rest of the world? While many pillars hold up our country's foundation, there are four that have significantly made America a great nation "under God."

THE PILLAR OF DIGNITY

Through the decades, human dignity, the worth of an individual, self-respect and the respect of others, and the value of human life have kept the foundation of America strong. President Washington warned of people who would labor to subvert this "pillar" of dignity, the value of life. Our courts have ruled that innocent, defenseless, unborn children have no right to life. To many, these precious little lives are simply globs of flesh undeserving of any human dignity.

Yet at one time we were the forerunner of the world in regard to human rights. All the wars in which we have been engaged have a critical common denominator: we never attacked first. My father fought in the South Pacific in the 1940s. Why? Because Japan bombed Pearl Harbor, starting a war that eventually cost America hundreds of thousands of lives and billions of dollars. A few years later, on the deck of the USS *Missouri,* the Japanese signed a peace treaty. And before the big guns on our battleships and the engines of our planes cooled down, American freighters were plowing across the Pacific to take the Japanese people what they needed to rebuild their nation. Why? Because we believed in the dignity of human beings and the value of life.

That belief is proclaimed by Emma Lazarus in words found on the pedestal of the Statue of Liberty: "Give me your tired, your poor, your huddled masses yearning to breathe free." King David's question echoes down the corridors of the centuries to today: "If the foundations are destroyed, what can the righteous do?"

THE PILLAR OF DEVOTION

One of the things that has made our nation great is our devotion to God, home, and country. We were birthed as a result of our ancestors' devotion to God. While not all the Founding Fathers were what we would call "born again," they were at least deists: they acknowledged the rule of a sovereign and supreme God who was above all.

Drive through New England even today, and you'll see a church steeple at the center of every little village you pass through. These buildings stand to testify that this pillar of devotion to God was at the heart of who we were and where we came from.

This is true not just in the ecclesiastical world but in the educational one as well. Each of our nation's oldest colleges were founded by a Bible-based denomination wanting primarily to train ministers. Harvard, founded in 1636 by New England Puritans, was once so ingrained with devotion that for several years their commencement addresses were given in Hebrew. Presbyterians founded Princeton in 1746; Anglicans founded Columbia in 1754; Baptists founded Brown in 1764; and the list goes on.

Sadly, schools today sweep their roots under the rug and promote a culture throughout the educational process that cannot display the Ten Commandments, and where prayer is prohibited. The pillar of devotion is being destroyed. People used to get a lump in their throats singing the national anthem at a ball game or from singing "Faith of Our Fathers" at a commencement service. King David's question: "If the foundations are destroyed, what can the righteous do?" is one we should all take seriously as more and more words like *patriotism* become forgotten words in our American vocabulary.

THE PILLAR OF DUTY

Through the years America has been set apart by the pillar of duty, by our work ethic. But, like other pillars, it too is crumbling before a culture that advances an entitlement mentality, where almost one half of Americans are receiving some type of federal financial assistance. The free enterprise system is what encourages ambition and incentive to work; the welfare system doesn't.

There is a dignity and a duty in a solid work ethic. Hard work has always been key to success and satisfaction in life. Again, we hear David's question echoing down through history to us today. Can you hear it? It is not a whisper, but a roar: "If the foundations are destroyed, what can the righteous do?"

THE PILLAR OF DECENCY

Common decency—basic morality—is also one of the attributes that has helped shape America, but our sense of decency has been radically redefined. I remember seeing the classic movie *Gone with the Wind* when I was a child and hearing Rhett Butler say to Scarlett O'Hara, "Frankly, my dear, I don't give a damn." The shock and rage that viewers expressed resulted in an uproar of condemnation. Yet today, many movies made for our youth are filled with expletives, and deemed acceptable. Major television networks show nudity without a word of complaint, and scripts are expected to be vulgar and vile. Pornography is now a multibillion dollar industry, and lifestyles that were hidden in dark alleys not that long ago now are paraded proudly down Main Street in most every American city, town, and village.

While the foundations are being destroyed, the church is too often symbolized by the answer to the reporter's question: "I don't know and I don't care." Ignorance and apathy are weakening the pillars of dignity, devotion, duty, and decency that made America the great nation it is.

One more point. Our neighbors to the north and south—Canada and Mexico—were discovered by explorers looking for gold and dominion. But the American settlers were looking not for gold, but for freedom to live out the gospel of Jesus Christ.

They were in search of God, not gold. They came to the New World, as stated in the Mayflower Compact, "for the glory of God and advancements of the Christian faith."

Q & A : *"If the foundations are destroyed, what can the righteous do?"* What shall we do? First, before saying, "I don't know what to do," look at the root cause of our problems. Then stop trying to apply political solutions to what are essentially spiritual problems. Instead of saying, "I don't care," begin to pray. Remember, we are the salt of the earth: we are preservatives. We are to be light in this dark world and take a stand for truth. Don't give in . . . Don't give out . . . Don't give up. Start saying, "I know!" and declaring, "I care!"

17

WHO MAY ASCEND
into the HILL *of the* LORD?

—PSALM 24:3

As King David penned this song of adoration and affirmation, he did so to celebrate one of the most glorious hours in ancient Jerusalem's history. The ark of the covenant was returning to Jerusalem, and the entire city was exploding with praise and joy. David himself was dancing in the streets in celebration. As the parade entered the gates of the Holy City, David began to sing:

> Lift up your heads, O you gates!
> And be lifted up, you everlasting doors!
> And the King of Glory shall come in.
> Who is this King of glory?
> The LORD strong and mighty,
> The LORD mighty in battle. . . .
> The LORD of hosts,
> He is the King of glory. (Psalm 24:7–8, 10)

Earlier in this psalm, David was more personal, asking, "Who may ascend into the hill of the LORD? Or who may stand in His holy place?" (v. 3). And no sooner did he ask, he provided the answer: "He who has clean hands and a pure heart" (vv. 3–4). This brief psalm is not simply one of celebration and commemoration, but also one of examination and anticipation. David took a backward look, an inward look, and a forward look.

A BACKWARD LOOK TO MOUNT ZION

Commentators are in nearly unanimous agreement that Psalm 24 looks back to the return of the ark (the very physical symbol of God's presence) to Jerusalem (2 Samuel 6:12–19). It is virtually impossible for any of us to imagine the degree of the Jewish people's awe and reverence for the sacred ark of the covenant. God had given Moses the design for this wooden box, overlaid in gold. It contained the tablets of the Law given at Sinai, a jar of the manna that fell daily from heaven to sustain the Jews in their wilderness wanderings, and Aaron's own rod that budded. The ark had initially found its home in the tabernacle in the wilderness, and carried by the Levites, it always went before the children of Israel. When it led them through the Jordan River, the waters parted. When it led them around the walls of Jericho, those walls came tumbling down. And between the cherubim on the cover of the ark, the shekinah glory of God would come to dwell among His people.

The ark had been outside the city and kept in the home of Obed-Edom for three months (vv. 1–11), and now David was bringing the ark to Jerusalem. Before he died, David would raise the funds to build it a permanent home. Later his son Solomon would masterfully and meticulously construct the temple in Jerusalem. There the ark would take up residency behind the veil in the Holy of Holies. What a day of celebration as the gates of Jerusalem were lifted up and the King of glory, symbolized by the ark, entered the city!

AN INWARD LOOK TO MOUNT CALVARY

Psalm 24 prompts us to look not only at Mount Zion but also to look toward Calvary. There is a strong Messianic appeal here: "Who may ascend into the hill of the LORD? Or who may stand in His holy place? He who has clean hands and a pure heart" (vv. 3–4). That "hill of the LORD" represents Mount Calvary, where Christ was crucified and died, an atonement for the sins of the world.

"Clean hands and a pure heart"—do you meet those qualifications? Can you ascend this hill? Can I? No mortal can do so. The qualification is twofold: one must possess clean hands and a pure heart. But my hands, representing my outward life, are not clean. I have sinned, and my actions and words fall far short of our holy God's righteous demands. And my inner life, my heart, is far from pure: like everyone, I have discovered that my own "heart is deceitful above all things, and desperately wicked" (Jeremiah 17:9). How will you and I ever be able to ascend the Lord's hill, much less "stand in His holy place"?

We will be able to ascend the hill of the Lord because of the one Person in all of history who met these qualifications: the Lord Jesus Christ, the King of glory. His hands were clean; His heart was pure. Knowing I was without hope, He descended from heaven so that I could one day ascend. His clean hands became dirty with the sin of the world, with my sin and yours. Why? So that our dirty hands could become clean. Jesus' pure heart became filled with sin. Why? So that my sinful heart could be made pure. No wonder we can wholeheartedly join the psalmist in this explosion of praise! No wonder we lift the gates of our hearts so that the King of glory can come in and take up residence within us!

A FORWARD LOOK TO THE MOUNT OF OLIVES

Psalm 24 presents us with a backward look and an inward look, but that is not all. This psalm also points to Jesus' triumphant return to Jerusalem. One day He will return, set foot on the Mount of Olives, walk down its rocky slope, cross the Kidron Valley, then ascend Mount Moriah, enter through the Eastern Golden Gate of the city, and, from Jerusalem, establish His reign over the earth. The watchmen on the gates will shout, "Who is this King of glory?" (v. 8). To which we, who are coming with Him, will reply, "The LORD strong and mighty, the LORD mighty in battle. Lift up your heads, O you gates! Lift up, you everlasting doors! (vv. 8–9). And the King of glory shall come in!" Through the gates and into the city once again Jesus will come, our conquering King of glory.

No longer will people see Jesus as the Galilean Carpenter-turned-Preacher, the Doer of some amazing miracles, and a gifted Teacher. Jesus will never appear like that again. Even now, He is seated on high at the right hand of the Father. And when He comes again, you will miss Him if you are looking for Him to be riding on the back of a donkey. He will be riding a white stallion and coming again as the King of all kings and the Lord of all lords. Our world is in desperate need of such a King who will rule in absolute righteousness and whose reign will stretch to the ends of the earth, with Jerusalem being the capital of the world for a thousand years of peace (Revelation 20:1–11).

Then when time is no more, we will hear for a final time, "Lift up your heads, O you gates." And an enormous multitude that no man can number will arrive with our King at the gate of heaven, and the King of glory will come in . . . accompanied by anyone and everyone who has looked to Him by faith for their eternal salvation.

Q & A: *"Who may ascend into the hill of the Lord?"* Only one Person in all of history has met the qualifications, and that would be Jesus. Represented in an earlier era by the ark of the covenant that was carried into the city, Jesus climbed the hill into Jerusalem with the express reason of ascending Mount Calvary. There, His clean hands and pure heart were stained by our sin so that our hands could be clean and our hearts pure. So who shall ascend into the hill of the Lord? You and I can—*if* we open the gates of our hearts and let the King of glory enter in!

18

How Can *a* Young Man Cleanse His Way?

—PSALM 119:9

*T*he times? They are a changin'," says the old adage. Today, relativism runs rampant, and sexual permissiveness and perversion are the norm. So of course it is increasingly more difficult for young people to keep their way pure. As I write these words, my mind races back to my own childhood and adolescence. I grew up watching television shows like *Father Knows Best*, *I Love Lucy*, and *Leave It to Beaver*. They consisted of a traditional family—a father, a mother, and children. They taught valuable life lessons like honoring those in authority and respecting the rights and property of others.

Young people today are also watching television, but their favorite programs have been *Seinfeld*, *Friends*, and *Modern Family*. Family television today features relationships, verbal exchanges, and sexual escapades that were only whispered about in days gone by. Media today offers few, if any, examples of a healthy and wholesome nuclear family. So-called family movies today are often sordid, sad, and empty. Tragically, many leave the movie theater to act out their own fantasies. We cannot find much that edifies in our current media or culture.

Again, it is a challenge in these modern times for any young adult to keep pure in mind, motive, and morals. Sex education in schools begins at an early age with little or no mention of abstinence. The urbanization of America has driven more people to highly populated areas, and for many young people, that relocating has brought anonymity and loneliness. Elementary-age children go home from school to an empty house and watch television shows filled with explicit sexual encounters and overtones. Good role models for the masses are not to be found. And then there is the constant drip of advertising that's directed at young people, and the movie industry capitalizes on this. Sex sells in this modern age of consumerism.

Although our culture continues to deteriorate, the answer to the psalmist's question, "How can a young man cleanse his way?" is the same now as when the psalm was written. The answer is constant and unwavering. It has never changed, and it will never change. The answer has three parts.

KNOW THE WORD

How can one keep pure in a world of perversion? "By taking heed according to Your word. . . . Let me not wander from Your commandments" (Psalm 119:9–10). It is virtually impossible, however, for the Bible to impact our lives if we know little about it. So the first step in overcoming a corrupting culture is to know what the Bible says. This bestselling book of all time will do you little good if you don't know what's in it or how to apply its teachings to life. I shudder to think what would happen in the average church if, on a Sunday morning, the pastor asked the people to turn to the book of Hezekiah. (Don't look for it. It's not there!)

Every believer should be able to give an answer to three vital matters in Scripture, beginning with *the inerrancy of the Word of God*. The Bible says, "All Scripture is given by inspiration of God, and is profitable for doctrine, for reproof, for correction, for instruction in righteousness, that the man of God may be complete, thoroughly equipped for every good work" (2 Timothy 3:16–17). Second, *the deity of Christ* is an essential and basic truth. The Bible says, "In the beginning was the Word, and the Word was with God, and the Word *was* God" (John 1:1, emphasis added). Third, believers should be able to explain *the means of salvation*: "For by grace you have been saved through faith, and that not of yourselves; it is the gift of God" (Ephesians 2:8).

So the first step in keeping oneself pure is knowing the Word of God. Read it and study it . . . daily.

STOW THE WORD

It is not enough to know the truths and teachings of God's Word in our head; we need to stow God's Word in our hearts. The psalmist answered his own question: "How can a young man cleanse his way? . . . Your word I have hidden in my heart, that I might not sin against You" (Psalm 119:9, 11). Knowing God's Word was Joshua's secret weapon when he led God's chosen people through the Jordan into the promised land. He challenged them, saying, "This Book of the Law shall not depart from your mouth, but you shall meditate in it day and night, that you may observe to do according to all that is written in it" (Joshua 1:8).

When we memorize and meditate on God's Word, we are able to take the Bible with us in all the traffic patterns of life without actually carrying it. This discipline brings with it a mysterious yet very logical outcome: "that I might not sin against God." Dwight L. Moody, founder of the Moody Bible Institute, wrote these words in the flyleaf of his Bible: "The Bible will keep me from sin, or sin will keep me from the Bible."

How can a young man cleanse his way and keep his way pure? He must *know* God's Word in his head and *stow* that holy Word in his heart through memorization and meditation. Knowing this, the psalmist added, "With my whole heart I have sought You; oh, let me not wander from Your commandments" (Psalm 119:10).

SHOW THE WORD

There is a third response to the psalmist's own question: showing the Word through our life and speaking it with our lips ("With my lips I have declared all the judgments of Your mouth" [Psalm 119:13]) supernaturally empowers us to keep pure in mind and morals. Knowing the Word will give you a knowledge *about* God; showing it through obedience will give you a knowledge *of* God. And there is an eternity of difference between the two.

We must put the Word into practice through our lives, as

Joshua said, in order "to *do* according to all that is written in it" (Joshua 1:8, emphasis added). You can never learn to play a musical instrument by simply memorizing the score and continually listening to your instructor play the instrument. The only way you can learn to play it yourself is to play it . . . over and over and over. It is better to *do* one Bible lesson than to *hear* a thousand of them.

So how can a young man keep his way pure? "By taking heed according to God's Word" (Psalm 119:9). In a culture where moral values continue to disintegrate around us, there is a surefire way to overcome: Know the Word. Stow the Word. And then show the Word in your life and with your lips.

When you find yourself at temptation's corner, trying to decide which way to turn, ask yourself these three questions:

- Can I thank God for it? "In everything give thanks; for this is the will of God in Christ Jesus for you" (1 Thessalonians 5:18).
- Can I do it in Jesus' name? "Whatever you do in word or deed, do all in the name of the Lord Jesus" (Colossians 3:17).
- Can I do it for God's glory? "Whether you eat or drink, or whatever you do, do it all to the glory of God" (1 Corinthians 10:31).

Q & A : *"How can a young man cleanse his way?"* In and of ourselves, we can't; it is impossible. But God provides the way with His Word. So *know* it . . . study it . . . learn it . . . fill your mind with it. *Stow* it . . . in your heart through memorization and meditation. Then *show* it . . . in your life and lips. Then, as Joshua 1:8 declares, "you will make your way prosperous, and then you will have good success."

19

WHERE CAN I
GO *from* YOUR SPIRIT?

—PSALM 139:7

*T*his question comes from the heart of King David as he meditates on the greatness of our God. The twenty-four verses of Psalm 139 are filled with his wonder at the depths of God's omniscience, His omnipresence, and His omnipotence.

Recently our young grandchildren visited us, and I marvel at their sense of wonder and inquisitive little minds about the world around them. It won't be long before they have passed through this stage into the cold, practical world of scientific explanations. Unfortunately, our wonder has a tendency to get lost in all of our sophistication and progress, yet every new scientific discovery reveals yet another reason to wonder at our amazing Creator God. As someone has observed, it is tragic that, in the service of God, too many people lose the wonder of it in the work of it.

David hadn't lost his sense of wonder. In Psalm 139 he expressed heartfelt wonder at our God—who knows all; who is everywhere present; and who is all powerful.

THERE IS THE WONDER OF THE LORD'S OMNISCIENCE

This big word simply means that God knows everything. Five

times in this psalm, David stated that God knew him. He began by saying, "O LORD, You have searched me and known me. You know my sitting down and my rising up. . . . [You] are acquainted with all my ways. For there is not a word on my tongue, but . . . You know it altogether" (Psalm 139:1–4).

So what does God know? He knows what you do. He knows what you think. He knows where you go. He knows what you say. He knows what you need. When David tried to grasp the extent of this knowledge, he became overwhelmed. Paul responded in a similar way: "Oh, the depth of the riches both of the wisdom and knowledge of God! How unsearchable are His judgments and His ways past finding out! . . . For of Him and through Him and to Him are all things, to whom be glory forever" (Romans 11:33–36).

What a wonder! God knows *you* . . . your e-mail address . . . your phone number . . . your worries . . . your hurts . . . your fears . . . your dreams. And He loves you.

THERE IS THE WONDER OF THE LORD'S OMNIPRESENCE

This big word means God is everywhere. Wondering at this truth, David asked, "Where can I go from Your Spirit?" (Psalm 139:7). First he tried the heights and depths, but he discovered God was there: "If I ascend into heaven, You are there; if I make my bed in hell [*sheol*, the realm of the dead], behold, You are there" (v. 8). From daylight to dark, from east to west, David could go nowhere that God was not present.

No matter where we are, God is there. Jonah attempted

to flee from God's presence. But to no avail. Adam and Eve tried to hide from God in the cool of the garden. But, again, to no avail. Isaiah's prophecy that the coming Messiah would be called "Immanuel," meaning "God with us," underscores this wonder-full truth that He is always with us (Isaiah 7:14). Where can we go from God's presence? There is not a corner of this big world where He is not present.

Because God is always present, we are never alone. And this assurance of His presence brought comfort and hope to the apostle Paul in some of his darkest hours. On more than one occasion Paul described how the Lord stood by him or with him (Acts 23:11; 2 Timothy 4:16–18). God's constant presence with us is indeed a wonder. He knows you, and He is always near.

THERE IS THE WONDER OF THE LORD'S OMNIPOTENCE

This third big word simply means our God is all powerful. Although David could have described the awesomeness of God's power in a variety of ways, he chose to focus on the miracle of conception and birth. Talk about a wonder!

> For You formed my inward parts;
> You covered me in my mother's womb.
> I will praise You, for I am fearfully and wonderfully
>   made. . . .
> My frame was not hidden from You,
> When I was made in secret,

And skillfully wrought in the lowest parts of the
    earth.
Your eyes saw my substance, being yet unformed.
And in Your book they all were written,
The days fashioned for me,
When as yet there were none of them.

—PSALM 139:13–16

Think for a moment about this wonder of wonders. David described two microscopic pieces of protoplasm that come together and form a live human being with all the intricacies of a nervous system, a respiratory system, a circulatory system, a digestive system, a mind, a heart, a soul. What a testimony to the omnipotence of our loving God who Himself "formed" us in our mother's womb! As I wonder at this miracle of birth, I can't keep silent about the harsh reality that our once-Christian nation has legalized the murder of millions of innocent babies.

After describing this wondrous aspect of God's omnipotence—the conception of a child—David praised his Creator: "I will praise You, for I am fearfully and wonderfully made" (v. 14). God knows us. He is with us. He is all powerful.

Having basked in the wonder of God, David ended this psalm on a note of vulnerability that is commendable and worth emulating:

Search me, O God, and know my heart;
Try me, and know my anxieties;

And see if there is any wicked way in me,
And lead me in the way everlasting.

—PSALM 139:23–24

Once we have caught the wonder of our omniscient, omni-present, and omnipotent God, we will likely be moved to join David in saying, "Search me . . . Try me . . . Know me . . . Lead me." We could be in no better hands.

Q & A : "*Where can I go from Your Spirit?*" In a word, nowhere. Our God of wonder is everywhere always. And, wonder of wonders, He not only knows the number of hairs on your head, there is nowhere you can go from His Spirit. You are on His mind even now. "You have hedged me behind and before, and laid Your hand upon me. Such knowledge is too wonderful for me" (Psalm 139:5–6).

20 WHO CAN FIND *a* VIRTUOUS WIFE?

—PROVERBS 31:10

*G*enesis 1 records the divine creation of all we know in the universe. With the power of His spoken word, our Creator God brought into being all that exists. And after each of these great creative acts, we read, "And God saw that it was good." He created the sea and the land, divided them, and "saw that it was good" (Genesis 1:9–10). He made the vegetation and "saw that it was good" (vv. 11–12). He made the animal life and, once again, the Bible records that He "saw that it was good" (vv. 24–25). Then He made a man, and immediately from God's mouth we hear, "Not good!" More specifically, we hear, "It is not good that man should be alone" (2:18). God created us to live in relationship with Him and with one another, and perhaps the most formative relationship is that between a husband and wife.

After one's personal relationship with the living Christ, there is no more important relationship than the one between a husband and wife. In fact, marriage is so central to life that Paul chose it to illustrate the relationship that exists between Christ and His own bride, the church. After discussing all the various nuances of the husband-wife relationship in Ephesians 5, Paul said, "This is a great mystery, but I speak concerning

Christ and the church" (v. 32). My relationship with my wife, Susie, is to present to the world a vivid and vital picture of Christ's relationship with us, His chosen bride.

So this question should take center stage in the heart and mind of anyone choosing a life partner: "Who can find a virtuous wife?" (Proverbs 31:10). The writer of this question then described in detail this virtuous Proverbs 31 woman. She is Wonder Woman and Mother Teresa wrapped up in a single package. She rises a good while before day every morning. She manages the entire household and assumes fiscal responsibility for it. She nurtures her children. She does her husband good and not evil. She operates a successful business. She stays up late making clothes for the family. She finds time for civic duties, being a blessing to the poor and those in need. And every Mother's Day pastors parade her out in their sermons, so that most of the moms are genuinely depressed long before they get to the Sunday noon meal.

Yet, there are some things about the Proverbs 31 woman, listed here for all posterity, that we should note as we look for a life partner. It is a good question, "Who can find a virtuous wife?" You will know you have discovered her when you see three important attributes.

A VIRTUOUS WOMAN LEADS A BLESSED LIFE

The first thing to note about the Proverbs 31 woman is her *faith*: "A woman who fears the LORD, she shall be praised" (v. 30). This fear of God—her reverential awe of the Lord—is the real secret of her blessed life. She was a woman of faith, which she firmly planted in the Person and finished work of Jesus Christ.

Her *faithfulness* is also of note. The writer says that "strength and honor are her clothing" (v. 25). He says that "she does [her husband] good and not evil all the days of her life" (v. 12). Here was a woman whose very life was characterized by faithfulness: she was faithful to her Lord, to her husband, to her family, and to her friends.

Are you looking for someone with whom to spend your life? Find someone who leads a blessed life of faith and faithfulness.

A VIRTUOUS WOMAN LEAVES A BEAUTIFUL LEGACY

This woman was not only characterized by her faith and faithfulness, but she also left a legacy for her *friends*: "She extends her hand to the poor, yes, she reaches out her hands to the needy" (Proverbs 31:20). Here we find a woman who was known for her compassion and generosity to others. Her actions say much about who and what she really was. She has left a legacy for her friends that should be a challenge to us all today.

She not only left a legacy for her friends but for her *family* as well. The Bible records that "her children rise up and call her blessed; her husband also, and he praises her" (v. 28). She was devoted to her family and loved them with an uncompromising and unconditional love. She left a legacy. She taught them—and is still teaching and challenging us, so many centuries afterward—how to live and how to love.

A VIRTUOUS WOMAN LOVES A BENEVOLENT LORD

When we think of what this woman leaves, we not only think of her faith, faithfulness, friends, and family. We also think of her attitude toward the *future*: "She shall rejoice in time to come" (Proverbs 31:25). I love the translation that says, "She smiles at the future" (v. 25 NASB). The motivating principle of her life is her deep faith in and love for God that enables her to trust her future into His care. She rests in the fact that every aspect of her life is in His hands. Yes, "she smiles at the future."

And the Proverbs 31 woman—like you and me—has every reason to smile: heaven is a wonderful and beautiful place. God loves beauty, or He would not have made things on our earth, so cursed with sin, so beautiful. The apostle John got a brief glimpse of heaven one day as he sat in exile on the lonely island of Patmos. Consider a few of the details he provided: "The construction of its wall was of jasper; and the city was pure gold, like clear glass. The foundations of the wall of the city were adorned with all kinds of precious stones" (Revelation 21:18–19). It is no wonder that earlier the inspired apostle Paul had said, "Eye has not seen, nor ear heard, nor have entered into the heart of man the things which God has prepared for those who love Him" (1 Corinthians 2:9). Yes, the woman of Proverbs 31 smiled at the future—and what a future awaits all of us who know and love the Lord Jesus Christ.

Q & A: *"Who can find a virtuous wife?"* For men not granted the gift of celibacy, know that God has created someone to complete and complement you. That someone will be one who leads a blessed life, leaves a beautiful legacy, and loves her benevolent Lord. And, by the way, Jesus our Bridegroom is looking for the same traits in us, His chosen bride!

21 Whom Shall I Send, *and* Who Will Go *for* Us?

—ISAIAH 6:8

*M*illions of people will gather this Sunday in *worship centers* for a *worship service*. When they enter the building, a friendly usher will place in their hands a *worship schedule* to follow with the hope that their time will be a genuine *worship experience*. Traditionally, America has been known around the world for our freedom of worship as well as our work ethic in the marketplace and our enjoyment of sports and entertainment. However, these three—our worship, our work, and our play—have become grossly out of balance. In reality, many of us play at our worship . . . worship our work . . . and work at our play.

In Isaiah 6, we read about one of the greatest worship experiences ever. When Isaiah went to the temple that day, his worship experience led him to see not only God in a different light, but also himself and those around him in a new way. This fresh perspective also enabled Isaiah to hear the Lord ask, "Whom shall I send, and who will go for Us?" (v. 8). As a result of his fellowship with the Lord, Isaiah responded, "Here am I! Send me!" (v. 8).

Isaiah's worship experience is left for all posterity in order that we might truly know if we have worshipped God in spirit and in truth. We see from his experience that genuine worship will always result in upward evidence, inward evidence, and outward evidence of our encounter with the Lord. Let's look into Isaiah's experience and learn for ourselves how to know if we have truly worshipped God.

UPWARD EVIDENCE: SEEING GOD'S HOLINESS

The initial evidence of genuine worship is seeing the Lord in the beauty of His holiness. The angel choir wholeheartedly sang, "Holy, holy, holy is the LORD of hosts" (Isaiah 6:3). And this great and holy God is not simply some force, the Great Spirit, or the Man upstairs. He is the Creator God, the Lord of the universe, the Author of history!

It is significant that Isaiah began his account, "In the year that King Uzziah died, I saw the Lord sitting on a throne, high and lifted up, and the train of His robe filled the temple" (v. 1). King Uzziah was the tenth king of Judah. During his fifty-two-year reign, he sought the Lord, prospered his nation, and built a strong national defense. He was the only king most of Israel had known, and they trusted and depended on him. But now the nation was in crisis. Uzziah was dead. Gone. And maybe you've realized this: rich worship experiences often come during times of chaos and crisis. Perhaps your Uzziah has died, and you find yourself without that one person or thing in whom you had placed your trust. Such was the context of Isaiah's worship experience.

Isaiah said, "My eyes have seen . . . the LORD" (v. 5).

Everyone else had eyes for the state of affairs around them, but seeing beyond circumstances to see God in His holiness as Isaiah did is always evidence of true worship. Isaiah had seen that God was "sitting on a throne, high and lifted up" (v. 1). The earthly king was dead, but God had not abdicated His throne. He was still in charge. His robe filled the temple, signifying His greatness as the King of all kings. The angel chorus's refrain of "Holy, holy, holy" signified that He was different from everyone else, set apart, and holy.

Worship is not about us. It is not about what we do, what we sing, or what we say. Worship is about almighty God and His glory. Isaiah exclaimed, "The whole earth is full of His glory!" (v. 3). When you and I see God in His holiness, we have truly worshipped Him. This view of our high-and-lifted-up God is the upward evidence.

INWARD EVIDENCE: SEEING OUR HELPLESSNESS

Too often we judge ourselves by the wrong standard. We look at people around us and measure ourselves by how we're doing compared to them. We are instead to look at ourselves in relation to the righteous standards of God's own law. As soon as Isaiah "saw the Lord," he realized the hard truth about himself and confessed, "Woe is me, for I am undone! I am a man of unclean lips . . . for my eyes have seen the King, the LORD of hosts" (Isaiah 6:5).

Isaiah did not try to sweep his sinfulness under a rug. His response was closely akin to others who have seen the Lord in all His holiness. Job said, "I have heard of You . . . but now my eye sees You. Therefore I abhor myself, and repent in dust and ashes" (Job 42:5–6). When the apostle Peter witnessed Christ's majesty, Peter cried, "Depart from me, for I am a sinful man, O Lord!" (Luke 5:8). Upon seeing the glory of Christ revealed on Patmos, John "fell at His feet as dead" (Revelation 1:17). When we truly worship—when we see the Lord in His holiness—we immediately begin to see ourselves differently. We see our sinfulness and cry out to God for help just as Isaiah did: "Woe is me!" (Isaiah 6:5). After Isaiah confessed his sin, the Lord pronounced, "Your iniquity is taken away, and your sin purged" (v. 7).

OUTWARD EVIDENCE: SEEING OTHERS' HOPELESSNESS

When we have a personal worship experience with the living Christ, we may be tempted to join Peter, James, and John on the Mount of Transfiguration, build an altar, and stay there. But genuine worship always compels us to go down the mountain to serve those in need. The *glow* of being with Jesus enables us to see the *woe* that prompts us to *go*.

Only after seeing God in His holiness and seeing himself in his helplessness, only after confessing his sin and being cleansed, did Isaiah hear God ask, "Whom shall I send, and who will go for Us?" (Isaiah 6:8). Note Isaiah's immediate response: "Here am I. Send me" (v. 8). He did not say, "Here I am." That would have merely indicated location. But "Here am I" revealed Isaiah's willingness to serve. Then a passionate request followed: "Send me." God responded by immediately giving Isaiah his assignment: "Go, and tell this people" (v. 9). Isaiah had a job to do. Genuine worship always results in the outward evidence of going to those people who are without Christ and are therefore without hope. Yes, the *go* always follows the *woe!*

The next time you leave a worship service, ask yourself these three questions: *Have I seen the Lord in His holiness? Have I seen my own helplessness? Have I seen others' hopelessness?* If you are able to answer yes to all three, then listen closely. God is still asking, "Whom shall I send, and who will go for Us?" Then, just as Isaiah did, shout your response: "Here am I! Send me" (v. 8).

Q & A : *"Whom shall I send, and who will go for us?"* Since billions of people in our world have never heard the sweet name of Jesus, the Lord continues to ask this question. Tragically, many of God's people never hear, much less heed, this question because too often we play at our worship. Listen for God's voice. Hear Him when He calls you. Then in obedience, "go, and tell this people" (v. 9).

22 WHO AMONG YOU FEARS *the* LORD?

—ISAIAH 50:10

*P*erhaps no Christian discipline is as forgotten as the idea of living in "the fear of the Lord." Who is doing this today? Who among us could define what it even means to walk in the fear of God?

We are living in what has become a "no fear culture." A couple of generations have basically grown up without being given any moral absolutes. The rampant relativism that has resulted feeds the "no fear" mind-set. There is even an apparel company that markets to this ideology with caps and shirts with only two words emblazoned across them: *No Fear*. Tragically, even the church can be a place of no fear. Instead of the church influencing the culture, all too often the culture slips into the church and influences it away from the fear of God. And now we find ourselves living in a "no fear culture" where the thought of living in the fear of God is a forgotten subject. Thus, Isaiah's question is as relevant today as it was more than twenty-five-hundred years ago: "Who among you fears the LORD?" (Isaiah 50:10).

Without having God on the throne, without having a priority to honor and glorify Him, without living in a spiritually healthy fear of Him, we are allowing the New *Testament* gospel to be pushed aside by the New *Trendy* gospel. The New Testament gospel emphasizes self-denial, but the New Trendy gospel emphasizes self-fulfillment. The New Testament gospel is focused on Christ and His life, death, resurrection, and plan for man's redemption, but the New Trendy gospel is focused on man and his desire for happiness and purpose. These two gospels are in diametric opposition to each other. The question of Isaiah will never be asked among those with a new trendy mind-set.

However, a thread woven throughout the fabric of the Bible is this: every man and woman used of God walked in the fear of the Lord. Noah was "moved with godly fear" as he built the ark (Hebrews 11:7). The Proverbs 31 woman "fears the LORD" (v. 30). The same is true in the gospels. The young virgin Mary praised God, whose "mercy is on those who fear Him" (Luke 1:50). In Acts, the fear of the Lord is mentioned on practically every page. We read that the community birthed at Pentecost, for instance, "continued steadfastly in the apostles' doctrine. . . . Then fear came upon every soul" (Acts 2:42–43). The epistles are replete with the same theme. Paul said we are to submit to one another "in the fear of God" (Ephesians 5:21). And, finally, in Revelation, John told of a loud voice coming from the throne, saying, "Praise our God, all you His servants and those who fear Him!" (Revelation 19:5).

Yes, Isaiah's question is very relevant today. The Old Testament saints, the faithful mentioned in the Gospels, the members of the early church, the writers of the New Testament epistles—all of these people knew the importance of living in the fear of God. Why is it a forgotten subject in the modern church today?

WHAT DOES IT MEAN TO LIVE IN THE FEAR OF GOD?

Does fearing the Lord mean living in a constant state of fright or concern that if we say something or do something wrong, God will zap us with some big bolt of retribution? Nothing could be further from biblical truth. The most common biblical word for fear means to stand in awe before God with such reverence and respect that that reverence becomes the controlling motivation of our lives.

When I was a teenager, my pastor taught me to walk in the fear of God—and he carefully explained what that fear was and wasn't. Oh, God wasn't calling me to live my life in fear that He would extend His strong hand of discipline toward me if I didn't cross every t and dot every i just right. Rather, walking in the fear of God meant living so that He will not take His hand of blessing off me. Fearing God is to live with the conscious awareness of His presence, and wanting to do nothing that might cause God to remove His hand of blessing and anointing from us. Living with that awareness makes an incredible difference in what we do, what we say, where we go, and how we live.

HOW CAN WE BEGIN TO WALK IN THE FEAR OF GOD DAILY?

We begin at the place where we begin with everything in the Christian life: the Word of God. King Solomon answered this question well as he prophetically spoke on God's behalf:

If you receive my words,
And treasure my commands . . .
So that you incline your ear to wisdom,
And apply your heart to understanding;
Yes, if you cry out for discernment,
And lift up your voice for understanding,
If you seek her as silver,
And search for her as for hidden treasures;
Then you will understand the fear of the LORD.

—PROVERBS 2:1–5 (emphasis added)

In your devotional Bible reading, start noting every mention of the fear of the Lord that you encounter. You will be amazed by how often you come across that important concept. And every time you see that phrase, remember that this fear is not the fear that He might put His hand of retribution on you, but the fear that He might take from you His hand of blessing and anointing.

Q & A: "*Who among you fears the LORD?*"
Unfortunately, far too few of us who claim to follow Jesus actually live in fear of the Lord. Determine today that you will—like those saints all through recorded history throughout the Bible—learn to walk in the fear of the Lord. After all, "the secret of the LORD is with those who fear Him, and He will show them His covenant" (Psalm 25:14).

23   IS IT TRUE?

—DANIEL 3:14

*I*s it true?" This question emerged out of a cultural context not unlike ours today. Babylon had conquered Israel and brought back some of the brightest young Jewish minds to train in the way of the Babylonians. The king had set up a golden image of himself and decreed that all his subjects would bow and worship it. And like a bunch of rubber stamps, everyone did . . . except these three young Jews. Upon hearing the news, the king summoned them into his presence with this question: "Is it true?"

Tolerance is the password in today's corrupt culture. One of my own life lessons and sayings is, "You have what you tolerate." Think about it. We have today what we tolerated yesterday. Many parents can attest to this. They tolerated disrespect and talking back by their kids yesterday, and today they see a young adult who has no respect for authority. The process will continue: we will have tomorrow whatever we tolerate today. It is a fact—we have what we tolerate. Tolerance used to mean that we recognized and respected other people's beliefs and values even when we didn't share them. Today tolerance means something entirely different: it now means that everyone's values, faith claims, and lifestyles should be accepted and that all truth claims are to be treated as equal.

While we are screaming "Tolerance!" our lives are being tested. The same was true for Shadrach, Meshach, and Abed-Nego who lived according to inner principle, not by outer pressure. When their moment of crisis came, they stood tall and firm because their decisions were guided by the Word within their hearts, not by the external world system. As the morals of our culture continue to crumble, we believers should expect to hear this same question asked of us: "Is it true? Is it true . . . that you do not bow to the gods of this world?" These three young Hebrews are shouting encouragement to us across the centuries today. They are saying, "Don't give in. Don't give up. Don't give out."

DON'T GIVE IN

Your faith will be tested. Woven through Daniel 3:1–12 is the concept of *peer pressure*. It would have been easy for these three young men to give in and get lost in the ways of that time. After all, everyone else was bowing to the golden image. It is so easy to go along with the crowd as we tell ourselves that even though we are bowing on the outside, we are still standing on the inside. But look at what Daniel's three friends did. They were not at all low profile as they stood in the mass of others who had no character or conviction, who were bowing to the golden image.

I can hear those young men saying to us today, "Don't give in! Don't do it! Don't give in!" In our world of "tolerance," our faith will be tested as theirs was. And we too will have tomorrow the fruit of whatever we tolerate today. Those three young men found their strength in God and in one another. They stood together—and they stood strong. There is a synergistic dynamic that comes when we stand together. If one can chase a thousand, two can chase ten thousand. Don't give in.

DON'T GIVE UP

It is strange how pluralistic Babylon and pluralistic America point to conservative Bible believers as the most intolerant of all groups. Yet the reality is that the culture and world system are intolerant of us.

Upon hearing the news of Shadrach, Meshach, and Abed-Nego acting according to their convictions, the king summons them into his presence. He wanted to know "Is it true?"—and if it was, he would have them thrown into the burning fiery furnace. The men did not give in to peer pressure, and now they would not give in to fear pressure. Their answer is classic: "Our God whom we serve is able to deliver us. . . . But if not, let it be known to you, O king, that we do not serve your gods, nor will we worship the gold image which you have set up" (Daniel 3:17–18). I love those words "but if not." Their faith was not based upon God's performance but upon His person alone. The question is never about His ability: He is totally able! The issue is about our response to His sovereign will.

One more point worth noting: these faithful and courageous men did not ask God to deliver them. They were seeking His face, not His hand of help. They threw themselves on Him and His higher will for their lives, regardless of the outcome.

DON'T GIVE OUT

Once our three friends said they wouldn't bow to the king, they had to face the consequences. That meant they were bound and thrown into the fiery furnace to their certain and very painful death. God could have kept these faithful men—and some of us—from the fiery furnace experiences of life. But deliverance *from* the fiery furnace is not nearly as significant as deliverance *in* the fiery furnace. None of us are immune to trials of life. Our Lord said, "He makes His sun rise on the evil and on the good, and sends rain on the just and on the unjust" (Matthew 5:45).

What happens when we don't bow or bend from our convictions? We don't burn. When the king looked into the furnace he saw four men, not three. Now a quick math lesson. How many went into the furnace? Three. How many were seen inside? Four. How many came out unsinged? Three. If any of us find ourselves in the furnace experience of life, this is just a reminder that He is still in there with us!

Upon seeing the faith and deliverance of these three, the King himself declared, "There is no other God who can deliver like this!" (Daniel 3:29). The very king who had earlier commanded all his subjects to bow and worship his own image now bowed himself to the King of all kings and the Lord of all Lords. Good things happen when we don't give in, don't give up, and don't give out in the face of a culture gone awry.

Q & A: *"Is it true?"* While we may not be hearing this verbally, people all around us are wondering if what we believe and act out is really true. And they often find out as we are being tested. Those of us who are called by His name are being watched by the world. Don't give in this week. Don't give up. And don't give out. Remember, you will have whatever you tolerate!

24 Is It Right *for* You *to* Be Angry?

—JONAH 4:4

*I*t is one thing to become angry when bad things happen to good people. But in Jonah's case, his resentment turned to anger when some good things happened to those he considered very bad people. It is of little wonder, then, that God asked Jonah, "Is it right for you to be angry?" Jonah is to be commended, however, for revealing himself as he really was.

When seventeenth-century British military and political leader Oliver Cromwell sat for his official portrait, the one that would display his likeness for all future generations, he instructed the artist to paint him just as he saw him—in his own words, "warts and all."

Since that day, the expression "warts and all" has been used in the English-speaking world to refer to a true representation of a person, to reveal the weaknesses as well as the good points. Jonah, the runaway prophet, concluded his small book in the Bible by doing this very thing: in chapter 4, he pulled back the curtain of his heart to show his true self, warts and all. Most of us, had we been writing this book about ourselves, would probably have closed with chapter 3's account of the mighty outpouring of revival upon the city of Nineveh.

But Jonah didn't. He added another chapter and included God's rebuke: "Is it right for you to be angry?"

Jonah's wart was his spirit of resentment: he could not tolerate the fact that the Ninevites had received God's blessings. Jonah's own pride may have been a bit bruised because he had earlier prophesied, "Yet forty days, and Nineveh shall be overthrown!" (Jonah 3:4). But it wasn't. God spared them. So Jonah went outside the city and fumed with resentment. He had lost all sense of perspective and wallowed in his own anger . . . not because something bad had happened to someone good, but because something good had happened to people he considered unworthy.

Such anger and resentment can have their own devastating and destructive effects on us. They will destroy our peace, divert us from our purpose, diminish our productivity, and distort our perspective.

RESENTMENT DESTROYS OUR PEACE

One would think that after all Jonah had been through and after all the lessons he had learned, he would be praising God for sending revival to the people of Nineveh. Instead, we read that God's mercy "displeased Jonah exceedingly, and he became angry" (Jonah 4:1). The Greek word *angry* means "to burn." Jonah was fuming; smoke was pouring out his ears. This is the first by-product of harboring resentment and anger: it takes away our own peace of heart and mind. Conversely, evidence of one who is filled with God's Spirit is love, joy, and peace.

RESENTMENT DIVERTS OUR PURPOSE

Anger has a far more debilitating effect on us than on the one who is the object of our anger. It not only destroys our peace, but it also diverts us from our God-given purpose. Jonah's pride was hurt because he felt God had discredited him. He became so self-centered that twice in chapter 4 he said, "It is better for me to die than to live" (vv. 3, 8). The prophet didn't hide his self-centeredness: "It is better for *me*!" His anger caused him—as it does all of us all too often—to make decisions on a what's-best-for-me basis. No longer was he concerned about God's purposes in his life or in the lives of the Ninevites.

RESENTMENT DIMINISHES OUR PRODUCTIVITY

Twice we read that Jonah sat down (Jonah 4:5). Before, we found him taking God's message to the streets of ancient Nineveh, obeying God's commands, and powerfully preaching His message. He was so effective that the entire city came to God as a result of his preaching. Yet in the aftermath we find him just sitting on a hill outside the city, half hoping it will fall so he could say, "I told you so."

Look at Jonah. Like the four lepers we met earlier in 2 Kings who were sitting at the gate of Samaria, Jonah was now just sitting. The city was exploding with joy over God's great mercy, renewal, and revival, but Jonah was not joining in. And people filled with resentment are typically like this: they become touchy and quick to take offense. They always talk about their rights and seldom speak of their responsibilities. Why? Because anger has its own way of robbing us of our productivity and sense of purpose. We lose our sense of mission.

RESENTMENT DISTORTS OUR PERSPECTIVE

A loss of perspective is one of the most damaging results of resentment and anger. And Jonah lost his perspective on the goodness of the Nineveh revival. Jonah became obsessed with complaints about a small plant, a vine that gave him shade and then withered (Jonah 4:6–8). It seemed that Jonah could not have cared less about the thousands of people in Nineveh who had just repented of their sin and turned back to God. For Jonah to sulk about a vine at a time such as this was sheer folly, but this is what resentment will do. Resentment and anger shift our values and make us focus on ourselves.

Thus, God went to Jonah and asked, "Is it right for you to be angry?" (v.4). Some counselors might have said to Jonah, "You are absolutely right to be angry!" hoping he would get past his resentment by feeling justified in his anger. Other experts would say, "You are wrong to be angry." There are people today who thrive on being told how wrong they are; for some unexplainable reason, they love to feel guilty. But God did not condone sin, and He did not condemn. He simply asked, "Is it right to be angry?" And that question got Jonah's attention.

God responded to Jonah's anger with grace and pardon. This is amazing condescension. God might have offered a stern reminder: "I could have cut you off when you sailed for Tarshish. I didn't have to provide the fish to protect you. I responded to you with patience and now with pardon." But instead God confronted Jonah: "Should I not pity Nineveh, that great city, in which are more than one hundred and twenty thousand persons who cannot discern between their right hand and their left—and much livestock?" (v. 11).

Jonah's story ends there, without our ever knowing what happened to him. Did Jonah carry his resentment to the grave? The shadowy ending to Jonah's book is most intriguing and leaves us to our imagination. Perhaps it ends as it does because each of us can be like Jonah. Perhaps the Lord wants us to look at our "warts and all" so we can see God's grace in our own lives.

So did Jonah learn his lesson? I am convinced he did. And I think the fact that he didn't end his story with chapter 3's great revival is evidence of his growth. He went on to show us himself "warts and all." And, as R. T. Kendall has reminded us in his classic exposition, he let God have the last word.

Q $\mathcal{E}$ A: *"Is it right for you to be angry?"* The obvious answer—for Jonah and for you and me—is a resounding, "No!" Anger eats at us like a cancer while almost never affecting the one to whom it is directed. So deal with anger just as you would any other sin: confess it and forsake it. And let God's grace and pardon transform your perspective through new eyes. And, like Jonah, let God have the last word!

25   WHAT DOES *the* LORD REQUIRE *of* YOU?

—MICAH 6:8

*C*ertain dates on the calendar need no explanation and demand no commentary. Several of them are anxiously anticipated and warmly welcomed. One in particular is December 25. Not much needs to be said about what that date means. Another is January 1. And how about July 4? Without saying a word, you thought of hot dogs, apple pie, and fireworks, didn't you? Other dates, however, prompt a much more solemn response. I am thinking especially of December 7, November 22, and September 11. The mere mention of such a date causes our minds to race back to where we were and what we were doing when we first heard the news.

None of those dates in December, January, July, September, or November require anything of us, but that's not the case with another date. It needs no elaboration, but it is different because it requires specific action on our part: April 15! On that date each year, we are required to pay Uncle Sam for the privilege of living in the United States of America. And if we don't pay our taxes, we will pay penalties instead.

God is rich in mercy and full of grace, yet He requires certain things of us who are citizens of His kingdom. Sometimes we think that because our sins are forgiven, it really doesn't matter how we live. Wrong! And the prophet Micah, who wrote seven hundred years before Christ, understood that.

Micah is best known as the one who foretold that the coming Messiah would be born in the tiny, seemingly insignificant village of Bethlehem: "But you, Bethlehem Ephrathah, though you are little among the thousands of Judah, yet out of you shall come forth to Me the One to be Ruler in Israel, whose goings forth are from of old, from everlasting" (Micah 5:2). Micah is also known for his very practical teaching in chapter 6. The lesson comes in a combination question/answer verse: the answer is embedded in the very question it asks! "What does the LORD require of you . . ." His three-part answer immediately follows: "Do justly . . . love mercy . . . and walk humbly with your God" (6:8). These three actions are not suggestions. Nor are they mere options. These behaviors—related to our actions, our affections, and our attitudes—are "required" of each of us.

OUR ACTIONS

Micah taught in a culture characterized by idolatry, immorality, and outright rebellion against worship of God. In fact, it was a culture much like the one we are experiencing today in America. Micah boldly proclaimed that certain things are "required" of those who follow the path of the Lord. First, we are required to "do justly." And he was referring to much more than a ruling in a court of law—God requires that we are to live differently than those around us. Specifically, we should be both moral and ethical in our dealings with others. We should always honor what is right and speak up for those who have no voice.

Justice has become a popular byword among young evangelicals today, but Micah was emphasizing action over mere talk. It is not enough for God's people to love justice and to be cheering from the grandstands for those people working for justice. Each of us is required to "do justly," to put justice into practice. What a difference it would make in our society today if more of us began to "do justly," and rushed to the defense of those who are suffering in unjust circumstances and situations. Again, doing justly is a requirement, not a suggestion.

OUR AFFECTIONS

God also requires us as Christ-followers to "love mercy," and the emphasis continues to be on action, not thought. We are not simply to show mercy to others but to passionately "love mercy." *Mercy* is best defined as "not getting what we deserve," whereas *grace* is "getting what we don't deserve." Micah's instruction means that we are required to give people what they don't always deserve; we are to cut them some slack and show them some mercy.

When we see someone in a difficult situation, though, some of us tend to immediately think, *Guilty . . . until proven innocent!* We take the seat of the judge when our "love" for mercy should be compelling us to be Christ's hand extended to someone in need, whether or not that person deserves it. Susie, my wife, is one who truly "loves mercy," and she has always reminded me that our children most need our love and encouragement when they least deserve it.

Hundreds of years after Micah wrote that God requires mercy from His people, the apostle John wrote this: "Beloved, let us love one another, for love is of God; and everyone who loves is born of God and knows God. He who does not love does not know God, for God is love" (1 John 4:7–8). For the one who truly loves God, doing justly and loving mercy are as natural as water running downhill.

OUR ATTITUDES

Lastly, the Lord requires us not only to do justly and to love mercy but also to "walk humbly with your God," a requirement that clearly addresses our attitude. We are not to allow the perpendicular pronoun to raise its ugly head. Pride, the "Big I," is one of the greatest hindrances to receiving God's blessing. This was the beginning of Satan's downfall (literally) when he said, "I will ascend above the heights of the clouds, I will be like the Most High" (Isaiah 14:14). In sharp contrast, Paul's admonition says to "let nothing be done through selfish ambition or conceit, but in lowliness of mind let each esteem others better than himself" (Philippians 2:3).

Again, the emphasis is on the action we take in response to Micah's instructions. We are to *walk* humbly before God and others, and *walk* refers to how you live your life. Enoch "walked with God" (5:22), Noah "walked with God" (6:9), and so has every man and woman who have known God's favor.

What is required of us? Justice . . . you must DO it! Mercy . . . you must LOVE it! Humility . . . you must WALK it!

And Jesus is our ultimate example. Knowing that divine justice demanded payment for the penalty of mankind's sin, and even though He Himself never sinned, Jesus went to the cross to "do justly." And from the cross we see how He loved mercy, saying to those who had driven the spikes into His hands, "Father, forgive them, for they do not know what they do" (Luke 23:34). Did He walk humbly? Even on the evening of His betrayal and arrest—the evening of His greatest need—Jesus was on His knees, washing His disciples' feet (John 13:1–17).

Micah 6:8 is not a suggestion, but a requirement. So keep your hands busy: do justly. Keep your heart broken: love mercy. And keep your head bowed: walk humbly with your God.

Q & A: *"What does the Lord require of you?"* There is a positive action to take: *do* justly. There is a powerful affection to awaken: *love* mercy. And there is a prideful attitude to forsake: *walk* humbly with your God.

26 O Lord, How Long Shall I Cry, *and* You Will Not Hear?

—HABAKKUK 1:2

his question, asked by Habakkuk, was born out of a "burden" that consumed him. He faced a moral dilemma: how could a holy God—who had called Israel the "apple of His eye" (Deuteronomy 32:10)—now allow the pagan Babylonians to besiege and ultimately destroy the city of Jerusalem and take away the Jews into captivity? If we are honest, most of us have felt like Habakkuk. We too have been burdened by the seeming inactivity of our God. We too have bombarded the throne of grace with our own prayers for deliverance . . . only to feel as though they bounced back at us off the ceiling. Thus we too are prone to ask, "O Lord, how long shall I cry, and You will not hear?"

If there really is a God who is all good and all powerful, why doesn't He always answer our prayers for good and right things? Why does He allow evil and suffering? Here is the age-old skeptic's argument: *Either God is all powerful but not all good (therefore He does not stop evil), or He is all good but not all powerful (thus He cannot stop the evil around us).* That statement sounds so logical. If He is really all powerful, then He could eliminate all evil, pain, and suffering.

In fact, He could absolutely eradicate all evil in an instant. But suppose He were to decree that, at the midnight hour tonight, He would radically stamp out all evil. On the surface that appears a wonderful idea, but is it? If He did, do you realize that not one of us would be here at 12:01? How thankful we can be that "He has not dealt with us according to our sins, nor punished us according to our iniquities" (Psalm 103:10).

But God has done something about the problem of evil. He has done the most dramatic, costly, and loving thing possible: He surrendered His only Son to die in the place of sinful, evil human beings.

The book of Habakkuk contains only three brief chapters, but in them the prophet showed us that the real issue at hand is not one of evil, but one of focus. Habakkuk outlined the route from focusing *on* our circumstances . . . to focusing *through* them . . . and finally, to reaching the place where we focus *beyond* them.

SOME FOCUS *ON* THEIR PRESENT CIRCUMSTANCES

This is Habakkuk's consuming focus in chapter one of his book. Listen to him: "O LORD, how long shall I cry, and You will not hear? . . . And You will not save. . . . The law is powerless, and justice never goes forth. . . . The wicked surround the righteous" (Habakkuk 1:2, 4). His cry may have been yours at times: "Where are You, God? Why don't You do something?" He was asking what so many are asking today. He was asking what we have already heard Gideon ask in this volume: "If the LORD is with us, why then has all this happened to us?" (Judges 6:13).

When unfair circumstances begin to swirl around us, our tendency is to put our entire focus on our problem. It begins to consume our thoughts. But just because you are in a storm does not mean you are not in the middle of God's will. There are storms of *correction*. Ask Jonah. A storm was God's way of correcting his path. There are storms of *perfection*. Ask the disciples about a late night on the rough seas of Galilee. A storm was God's way of refining the disciples' faith.

When difficulties come and, like Habakkuk, we focus our attention upon them, it simply leads us to ask a multitude of questions that have no satisfying answers.

SOME FOCUS *THROUGH* THEIR PRESENT CIRCUMSTANCES

As Habakkuk moved into the second chapter, we see his focus changing. He started to look *through* his problem and no longer just *at* it.

The first step in directing our focus through our problems is *perspective*. When Habakkuk said, "I will stand my watch and set myself on the rampart [watchtower]" (2:1), he began to look at his circumstances from an elevated perspective, from God's viewpoint and no longer only his own. Joseph offered a good illustration of this. Nothing that happened to him was—from the human perspective—good. But down in Egypt, when he revealed himself to his brothers, who had betrayed him, he said, "God sent me before you to preserve life" (Genesis 45:5) and "You meant evil against me; but God meant it for good" (50:20). Perspective is the first step in looking through the storms of life.

Next is *patience*. Habakkuk continued: "The vision is yet for an appointed time. . . . Though it tarries, wait for it" (2:3). The true test of our Christian character may well be how we respond when we lose our blessings or, in this case, when we don't see an immediate and—in our eyes—acceptable answer to our prayers.

Patience is followed by the *promise*: "It will surely come!" (v. 3). In the kingdom of God, we live by promises, not by explanations.

Next comes the element of *participation*: "The just shall live by his faith" (v. 4)—yet this is one of the most misquoted verses in Scripture. It does not say "the just shall live by faith," but "the just shall live by *his* faith." The Lord is with us. We don't have the love, but He does. We don't have the faith, but He does. And He invites us to let Him share in His very being with us.

Finally, in focusing through the circumstances of life, there is the element of *perception*. Habakkuk saw that "the LORD is in His holy temple. Let all the earth keep silence before Him" (v. 20). God is still in charge. He has not abdicated His throne.

SOME FOCUS *BEYOND* THEIR PRESENT CIRCUMSTANCES

Listen now to how this man concluded his book:

Though the fig tree may not blossom,
Nor fruit be on the vines;
Though the labor of the olive may fail,
And the fields yield no food;
Though the flock be cut off from the fold,
And there be no herd in the stalls—
Yet I will rejoice in the LORD,
I will joy in the God of my salvation.

—HABAKKUK 3:17–18

This is the same man who, three chapters earlier, was shaking his fist in the face of God and blaming Him for his difficulties. Now Habakkuk's focus was beyond the present circumstances, and he came to realize why that recurring phrase "And it came to pass!" is on practically every page of the Bible: this too will pass.

On a given evening some time ago, I woke up in the night very nauseated. I went into the bathroom, grabbed a bottle of that famous pink medicine, and, just before taking a dose, noticed the red letters on the side of the bottle: SHAKE WELL BEFORE USING. From time to time the priorities of life find their way to the bottom of our own bottle, and our loving God comes along. Why? To shake us well . . . before using us!

Q & A: *"O Lord, how long shall I cry, and You will not hear?"* It may be that God has already heard our prayers, and we are unaware. Sometimes His answer is *direct*: we pray and immediately see the answer. Sometimes God's response is *delayed*. There are other times it is *different*: He answers in a way that is not what we expected, so we don't recognize it. Finally, there are those times when our request is *denied*. But the good news is—God always answers!

27   WILL *a* MAN ROB GOD?

—MALACHI 3:8

*S*uppose you asked me to write your biography. And suppose I had access to only one of your personal items to try to determine what was really at the heart of your life. I wouldn't ask to see your diary, even though I might learn many of your most private and heartfelt emotions, or your prayer journal, even though it would show me those people for whom you interceded and those concerns for which you regularly petitioned God. I wouldn't even request your Bible, even though I might find personal notes and insights you jotted down through the years as the Lord spoke to you during your private devotions. If I could use only one personal item to help me write your biography, I would choose your bank statement. Your canceled checks and debits would reveal more to me about what really mattered to you. After all, Jesus' teaching from a green and grassy Galilean hillside two thousand years ago still applies to us today: "Where your treasure is, there your heart will be also" (Matthew 6:21).

The Lord calls us to be aware of where we are investing the gifts He gives us. So, through the prophet Malachi, the Lord asked this intensely personal question: "Will a man rob God?" And God immediately answered His own question: "Yet you have robbed Me . . . in tithes and offerings" (Malachi 3:8).

THE QUESTION IS PERSONAL

Have you ever been robbed? I have. And let me assure you that you feel personally violated when someone unannounced and uninvited invades your private space—when he breaks your doors and windows, ransacks your drawers, and steals money and other valuables, often including irreplaceable items of great sentimental value. Only someone who has been the victim of such an intrusion knows the deep anguish it can bring. To say that being robbed feels very personal is a gross understatement.

Keeping that in mind, look again at what God said: "You have robbed Me!" Note the two personal pronouns in play here, "YOU have robbed ME!" This is a strong accusation, not merely an insinuation. The reality is, robbing God is like committing a robbery without a weapon. When we don't give financially, our Lord revealed that He is put in the same position of intrusion as though we were breaking, entering, and robbing Him personally. And the Lord's exclamation clearly suggests that our robbing Him pains Him.

Furthermore, when we rob God of His "tithes and offerings," that act triggers a chain of robberies—and we are complicit in each of those as well. When we rob God of His tithes, we rob His church of its ability to minister in His name. We also rob the world of the gospel by limiting many worthy and effective missionary enterprises. But on an even more personal level, we rob ourselves of great blessings, for "it is more blessed to give than to receive" (Acts 20:35).

Jesus Himself instructed us to "render . . . to Caesar the things that are Caesar's, and to God the things that are God's" (Matthew 22:21). Most Christians would never entertain the thought of not paying their property taxes, sales taxes, or income taxes: they know that this rendering to Caesar what belongs to him is right and good and required by law. And yet an alarming number of Jesus' professed followers seldom, if ever, render to God the things that are God's . . . and in the process they rob Him. It is personal.

THE QUESTION IS POINTED

God says, "You have robbed Me." We answer with a question: "In what way have we robbed You?" In a flash comes His reply: "in tithes and offerings" (Malachi 3:8). Some Christians today believe that the tithe (giving one tenth of our income to God) is an Old Testament command with no bearing or application on us in this dispensation of grace. The reality is that the tithe existed among God's people long *before* the Law was ever given. In Genesis Abram gave tithes to Melchizedek, the priest (14:20). Jacob vowed to give a tenth "of all that You give me" to the Lord (28:22). Later, when the Law was given, tithing was incorporated: "All the tithe of the land . . . is the LORD's. It is holy to the LORD" (Leviticus 27:30).

In the New Testament we find Jesus both approving of and practicing the tithe. The Pharisees were on the watch to catch Him violating the Law at any point, big or small. Certainly if Jesus had been failing to tithe, He would have had their stern fingers of accusation pointed in His direction. Note also that in His rebuke of the Pharisees, Jesus said, "Woe to you, scribes and Pharisees, hypocrites! For you pay tithe of mint and anise and cumin, and have neglected the weightier matters of the law: justice and mercy and faith. These you ought to have done, without leaving the others undone" (Matthew 23:23). In the language of the New Testament, *ought* is an imperative, a command. Personally, I have not understood, in light of the cross, why anyone under grace would give less than those who gave under the law.

God promises provisions both in quality and quantity to those faithful in their stewardship of the blessings He gives them. God says He will "open for you the windows of heaven and pour out for you such blessing that there will not be room enough to receive it" (Malachi 3:10). By definition, blessings from heaven will be quality, and the fact that God's faithful will not have enough room to receive those blessings definitely speaks of quantity and abundance.

As far-fetched as it may seem, our finances generally mark the condition of our spiritual pilgrimage. We are often no further along in our walk with God than the point where we have learned to trust Him with our tithes and offerings. One-third of all Jesus' parables have to do with our stewardship of the income and material possessions He blesses us with. God never emphasizes our giving; He always focuses on our receiving, even here in His instruction about the tithe. God said, "Bring all the tithes" (v. 10). Why? To support the church or missionary work? No, that's not what God says. At issue is

God's desire to open for us "the windows of heaven" and pour out His blessings on us.

So God presents us with a proposition: "Bring all the tithes . . . and try [prove] Me now in this" (v. 10). Do you see how amazing this is? God is saying to you and me, "Put Me on trial! Test Me! Try Me in this." This is one directive in Scripture that can be put on a trial basis. If there is any doubt as to God's desire to bless us, here is a way to prove Him. This is amazing condescension.

Q & A: *"Will a man rob God?"* I would rather be guilty of robbing the bank downtown than found guilty of robbing God. If you also want to avoid robbing God, pray about your own stewardship and ask God to guide, provide, and embolden you. Make your tithe your top financial commitment; let it take priority over everything else. Be as systematic with your tithing as you are in your business matters. Rest in the fact that you can trust Him. Then get started. Just do it. "Prove Me," said the Lord.

28 IF SALT LOSES ITS FLAVOR, HOW SHALL [*the* EARTH] BE SEASONED?

—MATTHEW 5:13

A young boy went away to summer camp for the first time. When he returned home, his mom asked him what his new friends thought about him being a Christian. He proudly replied, "No problem, Mom! Not one of them ever even guessed it!"

Humorous? Yes. But also tragic—and, unfortunately, too realistic. Many professed Christians go about the normal traffic patterns of daily life, and no one has a clue about their faith. In an increasingly decaying and decadent society, our Lord reminds us that we are the "salt of the earth" (Matthew 5:13). All too often, however, the salt does lose its flavor.

Jesus had a unique way of using the simplest, most common things to illustrate the deepest truths. He spoke of shepherds and their sheep, lilies of the field, and birds in the air. In this chapter's question, Jesus compares His followers to salt and warns us of the tragic result should we lose our flavor. Jesus says, "It is then good for nothing but to be thrown out and trampled underfoot by men" (v. 13). Since Jesus has declared you and me "the salt of the earth," it is imperative that we understand four major effects we believers should therefore have on the culture around us.

SALT PRESERVES

One of my fondest boyhood memories is of our family's annual summer trek from Texas to the hills of Tennessee where my dad grew up. We spent those days with my Uncle Lester and Aunt Idele, who owned a small one-room country store in the mountains nine miles out of Pikeville. Even as I type these words, my mouth waters as I remember the taste of their salt-cured country ham each morning. Those slabs of meat were stored in a large wooden box in a cellar behind their house. In the bottom of the box, a piece of ham was placed on a layer of salt, then another layer of salt and ham, and so on until the box was filled. That ham was perfectly preserved in the salt without the aid of refrigeration. That's because salt is a preservative.

We are living in a decaying culture, and when something decays, it falls apart. Many of our social structures that used to be sound and secure are rotting away. Marriages and morals are continuing to decay at a high rate. And Jesus said, "You are the salt of the earth." The only thing standing in the way of an entire cultural collapse are those believers who are truly preserving the earth by being "salt" in their daily lives before others. Salt preserves.

SALT FLAVORS

Food without salt is tasteless and flat. But when added, a little salt brings great flavor to a meal. Christians are to life what salt is to food. Authentic Christianity always leaves people with a good taste in their mouth.

Our Lord was never discouraged that His disciples were few in number relative to the masses needing to be reached. He knew it only took a very little salt to flavor a much larger mass. I thought about this recently when I was preparing to eat a large baked potato. I cut into it and ate a bite or two without any real satisfaction. Then I sprinkled a bit of salt over it. Relatively speaking, the salt amounted to very little in proportion to the mass of that huge potato. But the next bite told the tale—just a few grains flavored the whole meal. So often, as believers, we think we cannot have much influence by our meager actions, but it just takes a little salt to make a huge difference at school, in the neighborhood, at the office, or wherever we might be. Salt not only preserves, it also flavors.

SALT STINGS

Susie and I raised our girls in Fort Lauderdale, Florida, on the beautiful Gold Coast of the Atlantic Ocean. Any person who has ever gone into that saltwater with a scratch on their body can testify that salt stings! When it meets an open wound, that salt makes its presence known—and does so in a hurry.

When Jesus said we are the salt of the earth, He meant that our very lives should bring conviction to—should sting—the people around us. While it is important that our presence serves to both preserve and flavor a culture, there should also be an aspect of our presence that stings when it comes into contact with worldly actions and attitudes. Too many believers seem to think they are to be like honey and soothe our sin-sick world instead of being like salt that stings in order to convict. When our Lord called us salt, He meant for us to not only preserve and flavor our culture, He meant to use our example to convict others of their need for Jesus as they see Him alive in us.

SALT CREATES A THIRST

The owner of the local movie theater in our town, Jerry, gloriously came to Christ as an adult. A few weeks after his conversion, he stopped by to see me and to confess something about which he had become convicted in his newfound faith. He explained that he had instructed his employees to always add extra salt to every box of popcorn they sold. Logically, this served to make the people thirsty; they, in turn, would buy extra or larger soft drinks while watching the movie. Yes, salt has its unique way of making us thirsty.

Is it any wonder that Jesus calls us to be the salt of the earth? There should be that ingredient in our lives that makes people thirsty for what we have in Christ. When Jesus walked among the ways of this world, He attracted all sorts of needy people. The Pharisees repelled the publicans and sinners who were drawn to Jesus. Why? Because He made them thirsty for what only He could give.

Tragically, in our world today, the salt seems to be losing its flavor. In the words of our Lord, when this happens, it becomes "good for nothing but to be thrown out and trampled underfoot by men" (Matthew 5:13). Each of us who are called by His name need to begin to see ourselves as salt. *We* "are the salt of the earth" (v. 13). Little does our world system realize that the presence of God's people is preventing the final collapse of our civilization and ultimate judgment. We are the only ones who can truly flavor the lives of those around us, sometimes even sting them a bit, and make them thirsty for the Living Water that enables us to never thirst again!

Q & A : *"If salt loses its flavor, how shall [the earth] be seasoned?"* It can't; it will simply be flat and "good for nothing." This is the real heart of the issue. As more and more Christians retreat within the comforts and convenience of the church, their salt will lose its flavor. We are commissioned to go out and be the salt of the *earth,* and not just salt for the church. The lost are waiting for each of us to get out among them, truly being the kind of salt that preserves, flavors, stings, and makes them thirsty for Christ.

29 WHICH *of* YOU *by* WORRYING CAN ADD ONE CUBIT *to* HIS STATURE?

—MATTHEW 6:27

s someone has observed, worrying is like sitting in a rocking chair. It will give you something to do, but it will never get you anywhere!

Our pressure-packed world offers countless opportunities for anxiety, anguish, and, in a word, worry. No wonder many of us spend an inordinate amount of time worrying: we worry about something in the past that can never be rectified; we worry about something in the present over which we have no control; or we worry about something in the future that may not even come to pass. Looking back over my own life, I confess that most of what I worried about that might happen in the future never did.

Still, we will overcome our worries only when we understand this overriding truth: God does not merely *frown* upon worry; He expressly *forbids* us to worry. The following four principles may help you more easily resist the forbidden fruit of worry.

IT IS FOOLISH TO WORRY

Note the context of Jesus' question: He was encouraging us to look at the birds of the air. They don't plant crops or gather a harvest. They don't build barns or maintain storehouses. The heavenly Father simply feeds them, a fact that prompted Jesus to ask His listeners, "Are you not of more value than they?" (Matthew 6:26).

Instead of using a great soaring bald eagle to illustrate this truth, Jesus spoke of the little field sparrows: "Not one of them falls to the ground apart from your Father's will" (10:29). These tiny birds—two were sold for a single copper coin—are vastly inferior and of far less value than you and I. So it makes sense that our Sovereign Lord, who provides for the birds and who cares infinitely more about you and me, will also provide for our needs. As the late singer Ethel Waters used to remind people at every Billy Graham crusade, "His eye is on the sparrow . . . and I know He cares for me!"

> Said the robin to the sparrow,
> "I should really like to know
> Why those anxious human beings
> Rush around and worry so."
> Said the sparrow to the robin,
> "Friend, I think that it must be
> That they have no heavenly Father
> Such as cares for you and me."
>
> —CIVILLA D. MARTIN, 1905

IT IS FUTILE TO WORRY

Not only is it sheer folly to worry, it is also futile. To help us realize this, Jesus asked, "Which of you by worrying can add one cubit to his stature?" (Matthew 6:27). At first reading, this question sounds like a reference to physical height. But a cubit equals eighteen inches, far more physical height than the context of this rhetorical question suggests. *Cubit*, however, can also mean "duration of life." Worrying will not increase your physical size, elevate your standing in the community, improve your reputation, or—as Jesus taught here— add any length to your life. Our times are in God's hands. The psalmist reminded us that our days on earth were already numbered before we lived a single one of them or drew a single breath (Psalm 139:16). So what will worry do for you? Absolutely nothing. Worrying is futile.

One of my own biggest challenges when trying not to worry about a problem is to hurry toward the solution. But no matter how bleak a situation looked, Jesus never hurried to solve it. Not once in the Gospels do we find Him saying to His disciples, "Let's go! We have to hurry or we'll be late for the miracle!" Waiting rather than hurrying—learning to wait on the Lord—is essential to overcoming worry. Throughout the Psalms we are continually told to wait on the Lord. Psalm 130:6 says, "My soul waits for the Lord more than those who watch for the morning." Consider this comparison. First, we have to wait for the sunrise. We cannot hurry it. It does not rise any sooner if I move the hour hand on my watch. Second, the sun always rises. We never wait in vain for the sun. Every sunset since time began has been followed by a sunrise—and God is just as faithful as the sun He created. Those who wait on Him are like those who "watch for the morning." He is always right on time, and no matter how desperate we may be, we can count on God to rise and meet us according to His perfect timing.

Worrying has never solved a single problem. In fact, it has complicated and compounded many of them. Worrying does not empty tomorrow of its trials, but it often empties today of its triumphs. Worrying accomplishes nothing.

IT IS FRUSTRATING TO WORRY

In Matthew 6, Jesus turns our attention to the lilies growing wild in the fields that "neither toil nor spin" (v. 28). They don't punch a time clock or worry about how they look or what they wear.

Specifically he calls us to "consider . . . how they grow" (v. 28). Growth remains something of a mystery: How does a tiny seed ultimately become a beautiful flower? How does a speck of protoplasm, undetected by the human eye, become a human being with all the intricacies of a circulatory system, respiratory system, nervous system, digestive system, and the like? In winter a flower bulb lies hidden in the earth, covered over by a frozen mound of ice and snow, as if it were dead. Yet, when spring arrives, that bulb bursts into life, sprouting stalk, leaves, and blossoms. Jesus wanted us to remember that the same God of glory who watches over those lilies watches over you and me. How do those lilies grow? God does it! They do not toil or worry. In His hands, they are carefree.

The moment we cut a flower off at the stem, it begins to

die. Today it stands, radiant and gorgeous, but the next day the colors have faded and the leaves withered. You, however, are immortal, and you were created in God's image. No wonder He cares infinitely more for you than He does for the birds of the air or the lilies of the field. That being the case, choose to focus on Him. Worry will never take you anywhere except to frustration.

IT IS FAITHLESS TO WORRY

Jesus was very direct: "If God so clothes the grass of the field . . . will He not much more clothe you, O you of little faith?" (Matthew 6:30). This gentle rebuke reminds us that worry is a lack of faith in God's promise to protect and provide for His people.

The real test of our spiritual maturity is not so much our actions as our reactions. In fact, the entire message of this Sermon on the Mount has to do with our reactions. If someone asks you to go one mile, go two. If someone slaps you on one cheek, turn the other to him also. If someone asks for your tunic, give him your cloak as well (5:39–41).

One more thought about worry. Both faith and worry are reactions to the events of life. If your life is governed by Scripture, you will react to certain circumstances with faith. If your life is not governed by Scripture, those circumstances will have greater power over you, and you will understandably react with worry. Worry is not just foolish, futile, and frustrating. The most damaging aspect of worry is that it reveals our lack of trust in God and His promises.

Q & A: *"Which of you by worrying can add one cubit to his stature?"* The obvious answer is . . . not a one of us. Worrying accomplishes nothing positive. The key to being free of worry is making God our top priority. Jesus put it this way: "Seek first the kingdom of God and His righteousness, and all these things [provision for our needs] shall be added to you" (Matthew 6:33). Believers who have gone before us trusted that truth and sang, "Just remember in His Word how He feeds the little bird; Take your burden to the Lord . . . and leave it there!" (Charles A. Tindley, 1916).

30 WHO DO MEN SAY THAT I, *the* SON *of* MAN, AM?

—MATTHEW 16:13

*W*hen Jesus asked His disciples this question, they were quick to respond: "Some say John the Baptist, some Elijah, and others Jeremiah or one of the prophets" (Matthew 16:14). They had just come from Galilee where crowds had flocked by the thousands to see and hear Jesus of Nazareth. The disciples had listened to the views of the people, collected their own polling data, and found that popular opinion about Jesus was divided. Things haven't changed much. Two thousand years later people still do not agree on who Jesus is.

Consider some of the opinions then and now. In Jesus' day, some folks thought that the spirit of John the Baptist—the recently beheaded prophet and Jesus' cousin—had entered Jesus. After all, both men preached the message of repentance. Other people said that Jesus was a reincarnated Elijah, and the Jews regarded Elijah as among the greatest of the prophets and teachers. In fact, to this day people have an empty chair at every Jewish Seder meal in honor of Elijah. Still others thought Jesus was the weeping prophet, Jeremiah. And then there were those who said He was just another in a long line, just another "one of the prophets" (v. 14). Ask your Islamic friends who Jesus is, and they will say He was a prophet.

So even today one of the greatest challenges believers face is how people answer the question Jesus asked in Matthew 16:13. What men say tends to carry more weight than what God says. Most often the opinions of anyone and everyone are more highly respected than the convictions of believers in Jesus Christ. The proof of this is all around us. Pick up a newspaper and you will find an "Opinion Section." I've always thought how wonderful it would be to read a "Conviction Section." But we live in a world that is much more attuned to what men say about anything and everything than to what God says about how to live life. Television talk shows lead the ratings in today's media-crazed, celebrity-obsessed world, further evidence that we care more about what so-called celebrities and experts think than about what our Creator, our Almighty, our Sovereign God says.

This preoccupation with what men think and say—and the disregard for what God says—always results in two things: pluralistic compromise and political correctness.

PLURALISTIC COMPROMISE

A pluralist believes that all human beings are en route to the same place, but we are just taking different roads to get there. Muslims take one road, Jews choose another, Buddhists go on a third road, Mormons have their own road, and we born-again believers follow the road we believe the Bible outlines for us. In other words, popular opinion argues that we can choose from among a plurality of ways to get to heaven. Understandably, pluralism characterizes a society that is more interested in what men say than in what God says.

In an effort to reach those listening to men, some mainline Christian groups have taken their theological remote controls and pushed the mute button when it comes to such topics as the wrath of God, His judgment, the sole authority of Scripture, and the exclusivity of the gospel message. Ironically—and parenthetically—one seldom ever finds these same individuals challenging other religions about *their* exclusive claims. Have you ever heard a liberal pluralist speaking up against Islam's claims of exclusivity?

Pluralistic compromise results when what men say matters more than what God says.

POLITICAL CORRECTNESS

Another result of today's obsession with the opinions of men and women is political correctness. To be politically correct in our current culture, one must adhere to inclusivism. This view holds that God's salvation applies even to men and women who have not explicitly believed in the Lord Jesus Christ. Inclusivism argues that since Jesus died on the cross for all people, everyone is included in atonement for sin accomplished by His crucifixion and resurrection. Again, whether your personal faith is in Christ alone is irrelevant.

In Acts 16:30, a Philippian jailer asked Paul, "What must I do to be saved?" Had the apostle been an inclusivist, he might have answered, "Relax! You're already saved. Everyone goes to heaven." But Paul's reply was pointed and exclusive: "Believe on the Lord Jesus Christ, and you will be saved" (v. 31).

Why should we, as followers of Christ, be concerned about

pluralism and inclusivism? Because these perspectives—these value systems—can dramatically impact the perceptions and practice of our Christian faith. Pluralism runs absolutely counter to our doctrine, to what we believe, to the Bible's message that Jesus is "*the* way" (John 14:6, emphasis added). If we believe that everyone is going to heaven, and that people simply travel on different roads to get there, then what do we do with the doctrine of the virgin birth, of Jesus' sinlessness and His role as Lamb of God, of the fundamental teaching that we are saved by God's grace through the faith we place in Him (Ephesians 2:8)? On the other hand, inclusivism affects our duty; how we behave and our mission as God's people. If we in fact believe that everyone is going to heaven, then we in the church no longer need to work on evangelism and missions. The church then loses its sense of urgency and passion to reach a lost world with the saving news of Jesus' victory over sin and death.

Again, we are living in a world today that is far more interested in what people say and do than in what God says and commands. Aware of this, Jesus moved beyond His question of public consensus to the real heart of the matter. In His next breath He asked His disciples this question of personal conviction: "Who do *you* say that I am?" (Matthew 16:15, emphasis added). And that's the question we'll look at next.

Q & A: *"Who do men say that I, the Son of Man, am?"* The answer is the same today as it was when Jesus uttered these words: there is no consensus. What God says is most important; the truth He proclaims will matter throughout eternity. Man's opinions fade into insignificance next to God's infallible and eternal Word. Peter had the right answer to Jesus' very important question, "Who do men say that I, the Son of Man, am?" Peter responded, "You are the Christ, the Son of the living God" (Matthew 16:16). Have you joined Peter and made this great confession?

31   WHO DO YOU SAY THAT I AM?

—MATTHEW 16:15

*L*eadership books are a dime a dozen today. Step into any local bookstore or shop online. You'll see right away that books about leadership abound. Everyone has an angle. Some authors offer a key to effective leadership. Many writers have come up with a catchy title. But, basically, leaders fall into one of two categories: those who lead according to public consensus, and those who lead based on personal convictions.

Those who lead according to public opinion wait until the polling data is in so they can see their constituents' thoughts on a certain issue. Once they have this information, then—and usually only then—will they take a stand on an issue. This is true in every sphere of our lives. It is often more apparent in the political world with politicians who keep their finger in the air to see which way the wind is blowing. But it is also true in family life. Some parents lead by consensus in the home, and that is why so many kids today seem to be in charge of the home. Politicians, parents, and others who want a kinder, gentler leadership role lead according to public opinion.

In contrast are those individuals who lead based on personal conviction. Deep in the fiber of their being, they have convictions about what is right and what is wrong, and those convictions dictate their leadership decisions. Those individuals who lead according to consensus help their followers do what they *want* to do. In contrast, those men and women who lead based on their personal convictions enable their followers to do what they *need* to do.

It was on this very point that our Lord took His disciples away from the Galilean crowds. Thousands of people had flocked to them on the northern shores of the Sea of Galilee, and they had been expending themselves physically, emotionally, mentally, and spiritually. Thus, Jesus marched them twenty-five miles north, all the way up to the foothills of Mount Hermon, to the headwaters of the Jordan River. There, around a fire, they engaged in a conversation about true leadership.

THE QUESTION OF PUBLIC CONSENSUS

First, our Lord asked the question, "Who do men say that I, the Son of Man, am?" (Matthew 16:13). Do you see that this is a question about public opinion? As we've seen, Jesus wanted His disciples to know what people were thinking and saying about Him. We live in a world today that is still more interested in what men say than what God says. Then He asked His disciples another question.

THE QUESTION OF PERSONAL CONVICTION

Now Jesus' question was personal and direct: "Who do you say that I am?" In the language of the New Testament, the "you" is emphatic: its placement at the front of the sentence gives it significance and weight. Had we been there listening to our Lord that evening, Jesus' question would have sounded more like this: "What about you, you and you only, you and no one else, you and you alone—who do *you* say that I am?" How an individual answers this question has eternal implications, and this is the question each person who walks on this planet must ultimately answer. Is Jesus who He said He was when He declared, "I am the way, the truth, and the life. No one comes to the Father except through Me" (John 14:6)? He is still asking, "Who do *you* say that I am?

In our pluralistic culture, to say that Christ is the one and only way to heaven is akin to waving a red cape in front of a raging bull. People today are far more interested in what men say than in what God says, and we set ourselves up as a target for attack when we state the truth that Jesus is indeed the one and only way to heaven. Yet that is the truth, and we need to follow Simon Peter's example. When our Lord asked this question, Peter immediately replied, "You are the Christ, the Son of the living God" (Matthew 16:16). Following our Lord's example, Peter used the emphatic *you* and said, "You, Lord, and You alone, You and there is absolutely no possibility of anyone else, You are the one and only Christ, the Son of the living God."

When we, based on our personal convictions, insist that Christ is the only way to eternal life, we are accused of being narrow-minded. In fact, some consider those of our more theologically conservative friends so narrow-minded that a gnat could stand on the bridge of their nose and peck out of both eyes! But all truth *is* narrow. Mathematical truth is narrow: two plus two equals four, not three, not five. That is narrow. Scientific truth is narrow: water freezes at 32 degrees Fahrenheit, not 35 or 36 degrees. Geographical truth is narrow: on the northern border of Texas is the Red River, not the Sabine River. Historical truth is narrow: John Wilkes Booth shot Abraham Lincoln in the Ford Theatre in Washington. Booth didn't stab Lincoln in the back in the Bowery in lower Manhattan. So why should we be surprised that theological truth is narrow? Jesus Himself invited potential followers to "enter by the narrow gate" (Matthew 7:13).

Our religiously pluralistic world is much like the world in which our Christian faith was birthed. In Rome, one can visit the remains of the Pantheon, the temple to all the gods. It was there that the conquered people of the Roman Empire could go and worship the gods they had served, whether they were Jupiter or Juno or whomever. But the conquered followers of Christ refused to have a niche for Jesus alongside those for Jupiter and Juno. These early believers insisted Jesus is the only true God, and many of these faithful gave their lives for that truth.

Jesus asked, "Who do *you* say that I am?" Again, this is the very question each of us will have to answer on that day when we stand before Jesus, who died on the cross as payment for our sins. Public opinion will be absolutely irrelevant. What other people say will be of no help. *Your* own personal conviction is what will matter. Will you answer with Simon Peter's great confession when he boldly proclaimed, "You, Lord, and You alone, You and there is absolutely no possibility of anyone else, You are the one and only Christ, the Son of the living God!" (paraphrased).

Q $\&$ A: *"Who do you say that I am?"* In the early church the key question Jesus asked His followers was, "Will you lay down your life for My sake?" (John 13:38). And hundreds of thousands answered yes and died a martyr's death. In our increasingly pluralistic culture that affirms all truth claims as equal, the key question for believers today is, "Who do you say that I am?" Jesus did not ask, "Who do you think I am?" or "Who do you wish I were?" Jesus asked, "Who do you say that I am? What are you telling a lost and lonely world about Me?" We must rise up and answer, "You are the Christ, the Son of the living God" (Matthew 16:16).

32 WHO IS THIS?

*I*t was only a matter of days before He would be crucified, and Jesus had just entered Jerusalem. The crowd had been waving palm branches and shouting His praise. The onlookers weren't sure what was happening. In Matthew's words, "When [Jesus] had come into Jerusalem, all the city was moved, saying, 'Who is this?'" (21:10).

"Who is this?" This question does not belong only in first-century Jerusalem. Throughout the centuries and continuing today, people have been opinionating and speculating on the identity of Jesus of Nazareth. Some say He was a sort of guru, a wise and gentle teacher of trite platitudes and object lessons. Others say Jesus was one in a long line of prophets. And more than one apologist has argued that there are only three possibilities as to Christ's identity: He was a *liar*, falsely claiming to be God; He was a *lunatic*, bona fide crazy and delusional, out of touch with reality; or He was, in fact, who He said He was, the Son of God, *Lord*.

Jesus was not low profile when He entered Jerusalem. Matthew reported that when He entered the city on Palm Sunday, "all the city was moved" when He arrived (v. 10). In their puzzlement, they asked, "Who is this?" Do you desire to see God move in such a way that your own city is stirred and your neighbors begin to ask, "Who is this?" Who is this who put your life back together and made something beautiful of it? Who is this who restored your family? Who is this who delivered you from addiction? Who is this who turned your sadness into joy? *Who is this?*

What does it take for God to move, shake, and stir an entire city? We can learn from this singular day two thousand years ago. It happened when Jesus' followers began to *experience* Him, to *extol* Him, and to *extend* Him to others. The result? The people around them began to ask, "Who is this?"

EXPERIENCE HIM

We come to know Jesus when we experience being in His presence. And the way to genuinely experience Him is to listen to Him and obey Him. Such was the case two thousand years ago. The stage was set for the city to encounter and experience Jesus when He instructed two of His disciples to go into a nearby village, find a donkey, and bring it to Him. "So the disciples went and did as Jesus commanded them" (Matthew 21:6). No doubt. No defiance. No delay. They just "went and did" in obedience to Jesus, fulfilling the Old Testament prophecy that "your King is coming to you; . . . lowly and riding on a donkey" (Zechariah 9:9).

These two followers who were sent to get a donkey could have decided that a white stallion would be much more appropriate for their Master. But they didn't. They simply obeyed Him. Too many Christ-followers today, however, let what we think ought to be take priority over His actual commands. Yet one reason God moved the city that day to ask, "Who is this?" was the tremendous spirit of obedience among those who listened to Him. Jesus is still on His throne today, He is still speaking to us, and He is still commanding us to obey His commandments as set forth in His Word. When we honor Him by obeying Him, when more of His own people begin to experience Him through obedience to His Word, we will find that He is also still in the business of moving cities to ask, "Who is this?"

EXTOL HIM

As Jesus began His descent into Jerusalem, the people began to honor and extol Him. They literally carpeted the road with their coats and palm branches as they shouted their praise: "Hosanna to the Son of David! Blessed is He who comes in the name of the LORD! Hosanna in the highest!" (Matthew 21:9).

What brought about this outburst of praise? Put yourself in the crowd and you'll soon find out. Look over there at Bartimaeus. Just last week in Jericho, he was blind and begging by the side of the road. But then Jesus noticed him, stopped, and gave sight to his darkened eyes with a spoken word. Now Bartimaeus was seeing everything around him. No wonder he was praising Jesus! And look over there at that man with tears of joy streaming down his face. Why, it's Lazarus of Bethany, who not long ago was dead and in the grave . . . until Jesus gave him new life. And there, over there, is that formerly crippled man who for thirty-eight years could be found lying by the pool of Bethesda. But look at him now, dancing and singing and shouting his own hosannas to this King of kings.

Do you and I have any less reason to extol Jesus, to shout our own hosannas today? We have seen His greatest miracle ever: His provision of new birth through His death and resurrection. We were dead in our sin until He brought us new life. Yet, sadly, some of us have lost the joyful spirit of praise—and we desperately need to recover it. God will move in our cities and prompt those around us to ask, "Who is this?" when we, like those of old who have experienced Him—we who choose to obey Him—extol Him with our praise.

EXTEND HIM

Those faithful followers lining the street on that original Palm Sunday did not only praise Jesus, they began to extend Him to others. They wanted others to meet their Savior and Lord. Nothing could keep them from sharing the good news that Jesus was their long-awaited Messiah and that they had found in Him their hope. Enthusiasm filled the day.

Caught up in the excitement of this moment, the people began to ask, "Who is this?" And the crowd lining the street responded with, "This is Jesus, the prophet from Nazareth of Galilee" (Matthew 26:10–11). The people who had gathered not only experienced Jesus that day, they not only extolled Him, but they extended Him to others. "This is Jesus!" was their cry.

When we do the same—when we praise Jesus for what He has done in our lives and share our stories with others—the people around us will also ask, "Who is this?" Who is this . . . who transformed your life? Who is this . . . who put your family back together? Who is this . . . who brought you peace in the midst of such tragedy? Who is this . . . who enabled you to be victorious over your addiction? Who is this . . . who gave you hope in the darkness of your circumstances? Who is this? Who *is* this? "This is Jesus!" You have experienced Him, so now extol Him and extend Him to others.

Q & A: *"Who is this?"* Ultimately, each of us must answer this question for ourselves. Who is Jesus to you? Was He a liar—a figure out of history who made some outrageous and completely untrue claims about Himself? Was He a lunatic—some crazed prophet from the middle of nowhere with illusions of grandeur and delusions of deity? Or is Jesus Lord? Your eternal destiny rests on your answer. May you join with the crowd in exclaiming, "This is Jesus!"

33   WHICH IS *the* GREAT COMMANDMENT *in the* LAW?

—MATTHEW 22:36

*W*hat is your primary purpose? Everything has a primary purpose, and when it ceases to fulfill its purpose, it is useless. The primary purpose of a pen, for instance, is to write. I would rather have an inexpensive plastic pen that wrote every time I picked it up than an expensive German pen that didn't. The primary purpose of a car is to take me from point A to point B. I would rather have a less expensive but reliable car that started every time and always ran well than a shiny new one that started only half the time.

When Jesus was asked, "Which is the great commandment in the law?" He went straight to the heart of your primary purpose and mine. Without hesitating He replied, "'You shall love the LORD your God with all your heart, with all your soul, and with all your mind.' This is the first and great commandment. And the second is like it: 'You shall love your neighbor as yourself'" (Matthew 22:37–39).

Including the Ten Commandments, the Jewish Torah—comprised of the first five books of the Bible—contains 613 commandments. When the Jewish lawyer posed the question, Jesus used the phrase "first and great" to clarify that He was also taking into consideration the Ten Commandments. Jesus went on to say, "On these two commandments hang all the Law and the Prophets" (v. 40).

Loving God (the vertical dimension of life) and loving one another (the horizontal dimension) represent all that the Ten Commandments address. The first four commandments (having no other gods before Him, not making an image or likeness, not taking His name in vain, and remembering to keep the Sabbath day) have to do with our relationship with God, the upward, or vertical, expression. The last six (honoring our parents, not murdering, not committing adultery, not stealing, not lying, and not coveting) speak about our relationship with other people, the outward, or horizontal, expression. So, although the Pharisees were "testing" Jesus when they asked this question (v. 35), He simply told them that all the commandments boil down to this: love. According to Jesus, we who are His followers are to love God supremely and to love people around us. Recognizing the role of love in God's kingdom, the apostle Paul later wrote, "The greatest of these [faith, hope, and love] is love" (1 Corinthians 13:13).

THE VERTICAL DIMENSION

When asked to identify the "great" commandment of the hundreds of commandments in the Bible, Jesus emphasized that the "first and great commandment" is to love God with all that we are. To make love for God supreme over love for our fellow man is in diametric opposition to the world's ways. Humanistic thought tells us that the way to love God is to love man. It says,

"If you love man and are immersed in all sorts of humanistic, social experiments, you will be on your way to loving God." But Jesus said the opposite. He knew that we can never love one another as we should unless we love Him first and foremost. When we love God with "all [our] heart, with all [our] soul, and with all [our] mind," there is no possibility of not loving "our neighbors as ourselves."

Many years ago I fell head over heels in love with my wife, Susie, for many reasons. One, we liked to be together—and we liked to be together . . . alone. We wrote each other love letters and, separated by miles while we were in college, we spoke on the phone every night. If you love the Lord Jesus, you will want to be with Him. You will want to be with Him . . . alone. You will not just read His love letter to you, but you will hang on every word in the Bible. And you will speak with Him daily in prayer.

What is the greatest of all the commandments? It is the command to love God with every fiber of our being. After all, "God is love" (1 John 4:8).

THE HORIZONTAL DIMENSION

The vertical dimension of a life that honors God is our developing and maintaining an intimate, constant relationship with Him. The horizontal dimension has to do with our activity toward those around us. It is of note that in Luke's account, this question comes in the context of the story of the good Samaritan where our love is revealed in what we do for others (Luke 10:25–37). Genuine love is always expressed by action.

In fact, Jesus said, "If you love Me, keep My commandments" (John 14:15). And one of those commandments is to love one another.

Unfortunately, many of us have real difficulty obeying this second commandment, "You shall love your neighbor as yourself." Some of us are void of self-love and self-respect. When that's the case, loving others as we love ourselves would not be healthy, life giving, or appreciated by those we "loved." Jesus knew full well that we would face this dilemma. So for thirty-three years He showed us what genuine love looks like: He was the very embodiment of love. Up until then, the best we could do was live on the level of this old commandment of loving others as we loved ourselves. He showed us by His life that true love is unlimited, unchanging, unselfish, and unconditional. The very natural self-love we know all too well is the very antithesis of all those things. Therefore, on the night before He was crucified, Jesus gave us a "new commandment." As He was about to leave us, He said, "A new commandment I give to you, that you love one another; as I have loved you, that you also love one another. By this all will know that you are My disciples, if you have love for one another" (John 13:34–35).

This call to love is not merely a suggestion, nor is it an option for us to consider. Jesus commanded His followers then and us today to love one another as He loved us. To be more specific, we are to live and love one another with an unlimited, unchanging, unselfish, and unconditional love, just as He loved us then and continues to love us still. How can we possibly love like this? We can't. It is impossible in our own strength. Only if we love God above and beyond all else, only if we love Him with all our soul and mind, will His love, abiding in us, overflow through us to the people around us. Only then will we be able to love one another as He loved us.

Q & A: "*Which is the great commandment in the law?*" Jesus didn't hesitate to respond: "Love the LORD your God with all your heart, with all your soul, and with all your mind" (Matthew 22:37). Love is the oxygen of God's kingdom. Love is to be the distinguishing characteristic that shows we belong to Him. You have a single primary purpose in life, and it is—to paraphrase the words of the "first and great commandment"—to love the Lord your God with every part of your being!

34

WHAT WILL BE *the* SIGN *of* YOUR COMING, *and of the* END *of the* AGE?

—MATTHEW 24:3

*S*igns . . . signs . . . signs. Ever since the disciples asked Jesus this question, people have been looking for signs of His second coming. When I began in ministry, for instance, a book by Hal Lindsey, *The Late Great Planet Earth,* exploded the market place and sold millions of copies. Concluding that a biblical generation was forty years, Lindsey implied that since Israel (symbolized by the fig tree in Matthew 24:32) had become a nation in 1948, "this generation will by no means pass away till all these things take place" (v. 34). The implication was that Jesus might return by 1988 (1948 + 40)—but 1988 came and went without Jesus parting the skies.

And then there was the widely told story of an American hotel company that wanted to build a hotel on the summit of the Mount of Olives, but did not due to a fault line that ran through the mountain. This geologic discovery was assumed to be a sign of the Second Coming, because Zechariah had prophesied that when the Messiah comes, His feet will stand on the Mount of Olives, and it would "split in two, from east to west" (Zechariah 14:4). This story was repeated in sermons all across America. However, for the past few decades, anyone who has visited Jerusalem has seen the beautiful Seven Arches Hotel (formerly the Intercontinental Hotel) sitting proudly on top of the Mount of Olives and glistening each morning in the Middle Eastern sun.

Clearly, just like the disciples who asked this question of our Lord two thousand years ago, we are fascinated by signs of His coming. But you may not know that the Bible actually speaks of three major comings. First, the coming of Christ, born of a virgin in an obscure village named Bethlehem, was foretold centuries before the Baby was born. Next, the prophet Joel foretold the coming of the Holy Spirit, and that prophecy was fulfilled on the day of Pentecost when the Holy Spirit came to indwell the believers, never to leave us and to empower us for service. The third and only major coming yet to be fulfilled is the return of the Lord Jesus to Planet Earth, His Second Coming. Just as surely as He came the first time, He has promised to come again for His bride, the church.

There are thousands of promises in the Bible, but this Second Coming will be the climax of human history and the fulfillment of the last promise of the Bible: "Surely I am coming quickly" (Revelation 22:20). According to Scripture, several events will herald Christ's return, no longer as a Suffering Servant, but as the King of kings and the Lord of lords.

WATCH FOR A POLLUTED PULPIT

Jesus indicated that, immediately before His return, "many

false prophets will rise up and deceive many" (Matthew 24:11). There will be a turning away from the truth. As Paul said, "The time will come when they will not endure sound doctrine . . . and they will turn their ears away from the truth" (2 Timothy 4:3–4). We are living in such a day. Denominations are dying, and many pulpits no longer preach that Jesus is "*the* way, *the* truth, and *the* life" (John 14:6, emphasis added).

WATCH FOR A PARTICULAR PLACE

The Bible says that before Jesus returns, before that greatest event in history takes place, the tiny nation of Israel will be reborn as a major player on the world stage. After all, God promised to "bring back the captives of My people Israel" into their own homeland (Amos 9:14). My generation has seen both the miraculous rebirth of the state of Israel and its remarkable rise to prominence as a world power. For the first time since the Babylonian captivity (about 586 to 538 BC), the children of Israel are ruling their own country from their capital in Jerusalem. After twenty-five-hundred years of exile, the Jews are back in the Holy City. And we have witnessed this miraculous sign with our own eyes.

WATCH FOR A PECULIAR PEOPLE

Many long centuries ago Moses shared with the people of Israel his prophecy that "the LORD will scatter [them] among the peoples" and they would find no "resting place" in the world (Deuteronomy 4:27; 28:65). But Ezekiel spoke of a day when God would "gather [His people] out of all countries, and bring [them] back into [their] own land" (Ezekiel 36:24). While there remains legitimate debate as to whether the modern, secular Zionist state is the biblical Israel that was foretold, the fact remains that unusual things are happening among these "peculiar people," the Jews (Deuteronomy 26:18 KJV; Titus 2:14 KJV).

WATCH FOR A POWERFUL POLITIC

The Bible indicates that before Christ's return, a powerful coalition of nations will emerge in Europe from the ashes of the old Roman Empire. Daniel referred to this as "the ten horns" of the ancient Roman Empire (Daniel 7:15–25). From this new world order will emerge the essence of a one-world power with a common currency. Sound familiar? This prophecy seems to be happening—today.

WATCH FOR A POPULAR POLITICIAN

According to God's Word, shortly before Jesus' second coming, an electrifying leader will emerge on the world scene. He is called the Antichrist (1 John 2:18). This charismatic leader and speaker will promise a world of peace. He will be filled with promises. He will speak of freeing the world of war and tout solutions to the world's economic and political problems. Much of the world will follow after him. There have been many such leaders along the way, not the least of whom was Adolf Hitler in World War II. It could be that since Satan does not know the timing of the Lord's return, someone is always on the stage who could fulfill the role of Antichrist.

WATCH FOR A PLURALISTIC PHILOSOPHY

The Bible predicts that before this climactic event of Christ's return, a new religion will emerge that seeks to unite the world under one banner (Revelation 17:1–18). A new age of humanistic thought will seek to exalt man over Christ. This philosophy has already infiltrated the Western world through the media and much of the educational process. Pluralism is the new religion of the day.

Jesus said, "When these things begin to happen, look up and lift up your heads, because your redemption draws near" (Luke 21:28). In light of this verse and the events going on in our world today, it just might be time for Christians to stop looking for signs and start listening for a shout!

> For the Lord Himself will descend from heaven with a shout, with the voice of an archangel, and with the trumpet of God. And the dead in Christ will rise first. Then we who are alive and remain shall be caught up together with them in the clouds to meet the Lord in the air. And thus we shall always be with the Lord. Therefore comfort one another with these words. (1 Thessalonians 4:16–18)

Q $\&$ A : *"What will be the sign of Your coming, and of the end of the age?"* The stage is set for the only coming prophesied in the Bible yet to be fulfilled, the second coming of our Lord and Savior Jesus Christ, not as a Suffering Servant but as a conquering King. At that moment every knee will bow and every tongue will confess that He is Lord! The last promise found in the Bible is spoken by our Lord: "Surely I am coming quickly" (Revelation 22:20). Let us join John in praying the last prayer found in the Bible: "Even so, come, Lord Jesus!" (v. 20).

35   Could You Not Watch *with* Me One Hour?

—MATTHEW 26:40

For three years Jesus had spent virtually every hour with His small group of disciples. They had listened to Him speak the greatest words of truth and life ever spoken, and they saw Him practice perfectly everything He preached. They had watched Him heal the sick, raise the dead, and walk on water. He had poured Himself into them, preparing them to take His gospel—the news of His sacrificial death, His resurrection, and His total defeat of sin—to the whole world. Now, the midnight hour had finally arrived, and the time to step forward as the perfect Lamb of God had come. Into the darkness of Gethsemane's garden He took Peter, James, and John. They clearly saw on His face that "He began to be sorrowful and deeply distressed" (Matthew 26:37). Jesus even admitted to them, "My soul is exceedingly sorrowful, even to death. Stay here and watch with Me" (v. 38). Jesus, who had already done so much for His disciples, made this simple request in the hour of His greatest need.

Knowing His death was but hours away, Jesus went only a few steps before He dropped to the ground, lay prostrate, and started to pray: "O My Father, if it is possible, let this cup pass from Me; nevertheless, not as I will, but as You will" (v. 39). After a while, Jesus returned to the disciples—and they were sound asleep. Can you believe it?! Asleep . . . and in His greatest hour of need. Then came from Jesus' mouth this piercing question: "What! Could you not watch with Me one hour?" (v. 40).

Jesus asked this question of Peter, who would one day become the undisputed leader of the Jerusalem church. Jesus asked this question of James, one of the original "Sons of Thunder" (Mark 3:17) and the first of the apostles to meet a martyr's death. And Jesus asked this question of John, who after pastoring the great church at Ephesus would be exiled on Patmos from where he would write the book of Revelation. Jesus was not only asking them—these men who knew the Scriptures—to pray with Him but also and primarily to "watch." His question was, "Could you not watch with Me one hour?" Upon hearing this, the disciples undoubtedly thought of the words of Isaiah, the prophet who spoke of the watchmen on the walls of Jerusalem who "shall never hold their peace day or night" (Isaiah 62:6). Seven hundred years earlier Isaiah had spoken of the importance of watching and praying.

A TIME TO WATCH

In the ancient days, watchmen were posted on the city walls twenty-four hours a day. Watching for any trouble, they provided security to the people who worked by day and slept by night. These watchmen also repaired any breech in the walls. They were under divine appointment. God said, "I have set watchmen on your walls, O Jerusalem" (Isaiah 62:6). They had divine assignments. They were to remind the people of the promises of God. They were never to be silent "day or night."

Likewise, Peter, James, and John had the opportunity to provide Jesus with physical security as well as spiritual security during this hour that He prayed. The disciples could have alerted Jesus to anyone entering Gethsemane, and more importantly, the disciples could have prayed for strength, courage, and peace for their Master and Lord. But the disciples did neither; they slept.

Do you hear and understand the note of astonishment, even disbelief, in Jesus' voice when He asked His question? First came the exclamation "What!"—"What?! What *is* this? After all you have seen and heard, after hearing just tonight of the bread and wine, My body and blood, what have you been doing? You couldn't watch with Me for one single hour?" There are certain times in each of our lives when our watching is far more important than any work we could be doing. Yet even in a season of work, we should always be like the watchmen on the city walls, keeping our eyes open to what is happening around us, our ears open to hearing His voice.

A TIME TO WORK

Reminded of Isaiah's words, Peter, James, and John would have known that Isaiah was prophesying about the return of the Jewish people from Babylonian captivity. On behalf of the Lord, Isaiah called the Jews to "prepare the way. . . . Build up the highway! Take out the stones, lift up a banner for the peoples!" (Isaiah 62:10). For seventy years Babylon had held God's people captive, but at the time Isaiah spoke, they were about to leave, about to return to their beloved Holy City. The several-hundred-mile journey would be long, difficult, and dangerous, and once they arrived, hard work would need to begin. Isaiah was calling God's people to *prepare the way, pave the way*, and *point the way* for believers who would come after them, and those three tasks were important to the disciples in Jesus' day, just as they are to us today.

PREPARE THE WAY

The Jews being freed by the Babylonians to return to Jerusalem would need to *prepare the way*, literally, for those who would come after them. God's people were to remove the rubbish, cut down the trees, and push aside the heavy stones in order to build a highway to Jerusalem, their spiritual home. God's people were to prepare the way home. Why were they instructed to pick up stones? So no one would stumble. There were folks by the thousands who would come after them.

PAVE THE WAY

These faithful were not only to prepare the way, but they were to *pave the way* as well. Isaiah used the words "build up the highway" (v. 10). The disciples' forefathers had made the literal way to Jerusalem easier, and now the disciples' generation was to make the way as easy as possible for those who would come after them. Why pave the way? God's finally-free people were never going to use that road to Babylon again.

They were certainly never going back for a visit or on vacation. They were already on their way home. So why pave the way? Because they were concerned about those people who would come after them. We in the twenty-first century need to be just as concerned about those believers who will follow us. What are we doing to pave the way?

POINT THE WAY

But preparing and paving the way weren't all the Jews were to do—or what we're to do today. Those Jews of old were also to *point the way*, to "lift up a banner for the people" (Isaiah 62:10). The Jews who left Babylon made it much easier for those faithful Jews who would come after them. In the same way, it fell to Peter, James, John, and those early believers to hold high the banner that pointed people in their generation and future generations to saving faith in Jesus, and therefore to heaven.

Similarly, Jesus Himself has prepared the way for us. In fact, He paved the way to eternal life, to the holy and heavenly City of David. And today, as He points the way with a nail-scarred hand, He continues to call people to a saving faith in Him, saying, "I am the way, the truth, and the life. No one comes to the Father except through Me" (John 14:6).

Listen again to the sorrow in Jesus' question: "Could you not watch with Me for one hour?" Isn't it time we who name Jesus as our Savior and Lord took seriously this question He asks us? When, in so many places, the heart of the church has turned to stone and the pulpit is simply a dispensary of human thought; when so many of our educational systems are citadels of anti-Christian propaganda and blatant humanism; when the media loudly and persistently calls our children to godless lifestyles; when too many believers are quietly tolerating a dying civilization; and when at least some of us are hearing our Savior ask, "Could you not watch with Me for one hour?"—when all this is happening, isn't it time for us to watch, to pray, and to cry out to God like Isaiah, "Oh, that You would rend the heavens! That You would come down!" (Isaiah 64:1).

Q & A: *"Could you not watch with Me one hour?"* Before we are too critical of this slumbering trio, we should remember a couple of things. First, we too have willing spirits but weak flesh when it comes to serving Jesus (Matthew 26:41). Second, Jesus is asking us today to watch, pray, prepare the way, pave the way, and point the way for the people coming after us who need to know Him and the way to eternal life He has provided. Let's be found faithful. Watch . . . and pray!

36 MY GOD, MY GOD, WHY HAVE YOU FORSAKEN ME?

—MATTHEW 27:46

*T*he famous last words of dying men and women are most intriguing and, in many cases, quite revealing. Some people have left this world reluctantly. Elizabeth the First said, "All my possessions for just one moment of time." Voltaire died with these haunting words on his lips: "I am abandoned by God and man. I will give you half of what I am worth for six months of time." Others, though, spoke final words that reflected a soul at peace. At his execution Sir Walter Raleigh said, "So the heart be right, it matters not where the head lies." Dwight L. Moody put it like this: "I see earth receding, heaven is opening, God is calling me."

Arguably, no one's dying words have been more memorable or more quoted than those of Jesus of Nazareth. Nailed to a Roman cross, in agonizing and excruciating pain, He spoke seven times. After a long night of betrayal and arrest, illegal trials and false testimonies, cruel mockery and a bloody scourging, Jesus was nailed to the cross and dropped with a thud into the ground. It was nine o'clock in the morning, and He was still hanging on that instrument of death at noon when a strange and mysterious darkness covered the earth for three hours. Shortly thereafter Jesus died. He had, however, spoken from the cross three times in the morning hours, once from the darkness, and then three more times in rapid succession after the darkness broke.

Jesus' first word was a *prayer*: "Father, forgive them, for they do not know what they do" (Luke 23:34). Jesus died praying for others. What He had earlier preached on a grassy green hill in Galilee—"Love your enemies . . . pray for those who . . . persecute you" (Matthew 5:43–44)—He practiced on the lonely hill of Golgotha.

Next came a *promise*: "Today you will be with Me in Paradise" (Luke 23:43). He spoke this word in response to the thief hanging next to Him who recognized his own sin, acknowledged the sinlessness of Christ, and then called out to Him with "Lord."

Then came a *pronouncement*: "Woman, behold your son!" (John 19:26). Seeing His mother, Mary, standing alongside His disciple John, Jesus commended her into John's care. Yes, Jesus died taking care of others. Significantly, He referred to her as "Woman," an indication that He was now severing all earthly ties. He would no longer be her son; now He would be her Savior.

Then came the darkness that, after three hours, was pierced with the haunting words of a *prophecy*: "My God, why have You forsaken Me?" (Psalm 22:1).

And after the darkness, three quick words. First, a *plea*: "I thirst!" (John 19:28), revealing the human side of our Lord. Next came the *proclamation*: "It is finished!" (John 19:30).

The Greek word means "to be paid in full." Jesus didn't go to the cross to make a small down payment for our sin; He paid our sin debt in full. Finally came His last word, a *profession*: "Father, into Your hands I commit My spirit" (Luke 23:46). And Jesus died.

Our question in this chapter has perplexed believers throughout the centuries: "My God . . . why have You forsaken Me?" I doubt there is a sadder, more haunting word in our English language than *forsaken*. Many people know all too well the raw heartbreak that comes with being forsaken. Some once stood at a wedding altar and heard a lover promise to never leave or *forsake* them. That promise was broken, and now life is lived with the reality of being forsaken. Countless children who have been abandoned by fathers or mothers live for years in the dark shadow of being forsaken. But does God forsake His own people? Never! Did He forsake Shadrach, Meshach, and Abed-Nego in a fiery furnace (Daniel 3) or Daniel in a lions' den (Daniel 6)? No! Then why this loud cry, this strange question from the dry, parched lips of our Lord as He hung from the cross?

We are reminded in Habakkuk 1:13 that God the Father is so holy that He cannot even look upon sin. This truth is why, on the cross, the words of Isaiah 53:6 became reality: "All we like sheep have gone astray . . . and the LORD has laid on Him [Christ] the iniquity of us all." The apostle Paul put it like this: "[God] made [Jesus] who knew no sin to be sin for us, that we might become the righteousness of God in Him" (2 Corinthians 5:21). On the cross Jesus took our sin in His own body, suffering shame, hurt, humiliation, pain, agony, and death—the consequences that we deserved. God the Father could not look upon the sin His Son was bearing, so He turned away. Darkness enveloped the earth as Jesus fought our battle with Satan on the cross. His words "My God, why have You forsaken Me?" come directly from Psalm 22:1, as though Jesus, quoting this prophecy, was saying, "I will endure this separation so that any and all who come to Me will never have to be separated from God and will never experience the pain of being *forsaken* by their heavenly Father."

Is it any wonder the Bible says, "Thanks be to God for His indescribable gift!" (2 Corinthians 9:15)? On the cross instead of giving up, our Lord reached up. In place of giving in, He reached in. And in place of giving out, He reached out. What a Savior. And, yes, "Thanks be to God for His indescribable gift!"

Q & A: "My God, My God, why have You forsaken Me?" Why did the Father forsake Jesus? The simple yet significant answer is that Jesus was forsaken so that we might never have to know separation from God. Jesus paid in full our sin debt. He died our death so we could live His life. He took our sin so we could take on His righteousness. Jesus was forsaken so we might never be forsaken. Read all four Gospel accounts of the crucifixion this week and meditate on Christ's redeeming and radical love.

37   WHO IS MY NEIGHBOR?

—LUKE 10:29

*W*ho is my neighbor?" With the fast pace of life today, many of us would be hard-pressed to even know the names of those who live next door. Gone are the days when we shouted across the white picket fence to borrow a cup of sugar. It is not just difficult; it is virtually impossible to love our neighbors as Christ commanded when we don't even know their names.

We all have our comfort zones. All of us have an easier time reaching out to certain people than to others. We all are more comfortable in certain social, political, religious, even economic circles than in others. So it is all too easy to get stuck in our comfort zone and never venture out to get to know our neighbors. Clearly, we can learn much from the man we have come to know as the Good Samaritan.

When a lawyer approached Jesus and asked, "Who is my neighbor?" (Luke 10:29). Jesus answered with a story about the good Samaritan. This man was going from Jerusalem to Jericho when he came upon a fellow traveler who had been beaten, robbed, and left by the side of the road. Some religious types had passed him by, choosing the other side of the road and rationalizing their decision not to help. But this Samaritan—a member of a race despised by the Jews—stopped, felt compassion, bandaged up the wounded man, and took him to a nearby inn to recuperate. Interestingly, despite this noble and good deed, Jesus never called the Samaritan "good." Jesus simply said, "A certain man . . ." (v. 30). Yet when we see someone who loves in this simple yet profound way, when we see him doing what he—what *we*—ought to do, we put a label on him to call him "good."

So as to the lawyer's question, "Who is my neighbor?" When Jesus answered with this often repeated story, He challenged us to leave our comfort zones and get involved in the lives of those around us who need help. Here are four steps He calls upon us to take for getting involved.

STEP 1: SEE THE NEED

This story shows that the process of loving—or not loving—a person in need begins when the passerby sees him (Luke 10:31–33). The priest and the Levite had noticed the same mangled man and chose to pass by on the other side of the road. Clearly, the priest and Levite didn't really *see* him with their hearts. The Samaritan, however, did see the wounded man, and his seeing prompted action.

Too often we, like the priest and the Levite, look at but don't actually see the people around us. Or if we happen to notice needs, we don't see clearly enough with our hearts to want to reach out. Jesus' story shows, however, that the initial step of loving our neighbors requires our vigilance: we need to commit to consciously see those around us who are in need. How often do we drive by dozens of people in need as we go to church to discuss and pray for people—especially for people on the other side of the world—who are hungry, lonely, sick, and living in darkness? We would do well to ask God to help us see the needy people who are around us—as this Samaritan did—with our hearts as well as our eyes.

STEP 2: FEEL THE NEED

Upon seeing the beaten man, the Bible says the Samaritan "had compassion" (Luke 10:33). His heart went out to the person in pain and in need despite the fact that—and Jesus made this very clear—the beaten man was a Jew and the one who rendered aid was a Samaritan. If that doesn't mean much, think of it this way. In modern terms, this gesture was like a black, liberal, dyed-in-the-wool Democrat seeing a white, southern, funda-mentalist, Tea Party member in need! It was akin to a member of the NAACP seeing a white supremacist militia man lying on the side of the road. The religious, political, and racial animos-ity between the Jews and the Samaritans was indescribable.

The Samaritan not only *saw* the need; he *felt* it. He had compassion on the beaten man, and such compassion fuels our involvement in other people's lives. Too many of us today are, like the priest and the Levite, too preoccupied, too self-centered, or too comfortable in our ways to stop and meet another's needs. We choose to walk by on the other side, per-haps pretending to be oblivious to the hurts and needs of our neighbors and clearly choosing not to help. The choice to be involved in other people's lives, the choice to help meet their needs, is rooted in one's heart.

STEP 3: TOUCH THE NEED

Having noticed the hurt man, the Bible says the Samaritan "went to him and bandaged his wounds" (Luke 10:34). It is not enough to see a need and feel a need. In this story, Jesus called us to reach out to touch and help the person in need. And in the situation Jesus described, the despised Samaritan took a big risk when he stopped to help the Jew. I wonder how many needs around us go unmet because we are not willing to take a risk as we travel our own Jericho Road. This Samaritan, however, did not let the risk or the cost involved deter him. He chose to take the risk and touch the need.

When God's people take risks and touch needs, His kingdom always advances. Abraham, for instance, risked leaving all he knew to go to a land he had never known. Moses took a risk and returned to Egypt, where he was wanted for murder, to lead God's people out of bondage. The young Virgin Mary heard an angel's message and risked believing it. Similarly, her fiancé, Joseph, risked believing that the child in her womb was conceived by the Holy Spirit. Talk about a risk! And the Samaritan risked answering the question "Who is my neighbor?" when he saw the Jewish man's need. He felt the need. Then he left his comfort zone and touched the need.

STEP 4: MEET THE NEED

This Samaritan could have passed by the bleeding man and, like the priest and the Levite, walked on the other side of the road. But the Samaritan didn't. Or the Samaritan could have bandaged the wounds and then left the man at the side of the road. But he didn't. The Samaritan carried the man to an inn, left him in the care of the innkeeper, paid his bill in advance, and promised to return in a few days to pay for any extra expenses. The Samaritan not only met the need for that day, but for the days to come, and promised to follow up.

Consider for a moment that each of us has been the wounded man lying at the side of the road. Jesus saw us beaten, battered by sin, and lying on the side of the road. Overwhelmed by compassion and love for us, He left heaven (His comfort zone), came into our world, and then touched us. Jesus took our old heart out and put in a brand-new one. Then, like the Samaritan, He took us to the inn—to a place of fellowship with His people—and promised He would come back to settle all accounts!

At the end of the story, Jesus asked which person was a neighbor to the wounded man. His hearers replied, "He who showed mercy on him." Then Jesus said to them—and to us—"Go and do likewise" (Luke 10:37).

Q & A: "*Who is my neighbor?*" My neighbor is anyone and everyone to whom I can be Christ's hand extended—and that definition includes people outside my comfort zone. I am to *see* the need—and not be blind to it. I am to let go of my heart so I can *feel* the need. I am to *touch* the need even if that means getting dirty. And I am to *meet* the need, following up after my initial response whenever necessary. In the words of Jesus, "Go and do likewise."

38   WHERE ARE *the* NINE?

—LUKE 17:17

*I*n America we once set aside a special day each year for the express purpose of offering thanks to God for His many blessings upon us and upon our nation. We called it Thanksgiving Day. Oh, we still have that day on the calendar, but along the way its original purpose seems to have been completely overshadowed. This special holiday has become synonymous with the parades and pumpkin pies, football games and food. Fewer and fewer of us pause to offer heartfelt thanks to God for His many blessings and great faithfulness.

One day, near the end of Christ's time on this earth, He was walking to Jerusalem when He encountered ten lepers in a colony to themselves. They began to lift their voices and call to Him for mercy, He stopped, spoke words of healing over them, and sent them off to the priest for confirmation of their wholeness. All ten had been healed, and nine of them immediately rushed home to their families. Only one of the ten men returned to thank Jesus, and He asked the healed leper—and us—a poignant and penetrating question: "Were there not ten cleansed? . . . Where are the nine?" (Luke 17:17).

With this simple question our Lord identified three actions that enable us to live life to the fullest. We should *get up;* this is a step of fortitude. We should *get out,* a step reflecting our attitude. Finally, we should *get back,* an action that reveals our gratitude.

GET UP!

If we don't get up, we might miss the Master. The Bible records that these isolated lepers got up, "lifted up their voices and said, 'Jesus, Master, have mercy on us!'" (Luke 17:13).

Do you get the picture? The Mosaic Law required lepers to isolate themselves from other people. They were forbidden to get within six feet of anyone—and if the wind was blowing, they could not be within fifty yards of other people. Should anyone be inadvertently approaching, a leper was to shout, "Unclean, unclean!" Leprosy was a hideous disease slowly eating away the flesh, erasing facial features first, then killing the extremities. The appearance of the leprous was ghastly; their odor, nauseating; and their death, long, slow, agonizing, and lonely.

All ten men in our story desperately wanted to be healed and live as part of their families. So when Jesus passed by, they showed great fortitude: they got up and called to Him for mercy. The lepers didn't need justice; they cried out for mercy. Perhaps as you read these words, you, too, are sitting beside a road. Perhaps Jesus has passed by time and again, but you never got up and called to Him. Be encouraged by these lepers to get up. If you don't, you might miss the Master.

GET OUT!

If we don't get out, we might miss the miracle. Not only did these ten lepers get up, they got out. They obeyed Christ when

He told them to go "show yourselves to the priests" (Luke 17:14). After the lepers were healed, the law required them to show themselves to a priest. When Jesus spoke these words, however, the ten men were still suffering from leprosy, still covered with sores, still forbidden to get too close to uninfected people. But what an attitude of faith these ten displayed: when Jesus said, "Go," they went—and "as they went, they were cleansed" (v. 14).

The language of the New Testament at this point is key: "As they went, they were cleansed" is in the passive voice, leaving no doubt that it was God, and God alone, who performed this miracle and healed them. All ten of them were healed as, in obedience to Jesus, they headed to the temple and the priests. All they had was the word of Christ. All they had was the promise of God's word. Yet they walked in faith and obedience.

Before every miraculous work God does, He moves us to the point where all we have is His promise, but that is really all we need. This is the faith life: "as they went." The lepers not only got up, but they got out, an act that revealed their attitude of faith. Had they not done so, they would have missed the miracle.

GET BACK!

If we don't, we might miss the moment. These ten men were lepers who called upon Jesus for mercy, stepped out in faith, and were healed. They all got up, and they all got out. But at this point the similarity ends.

Imagine standing with them on that road. Jesus healed them! Looking at one another, they were amazed and overjoyed. They jumped up and down and hugged one another. Then one said, "I haven't seen my wife in months"—and he ran down the road toward home as fast as he could. Another shouted, "I have never held my newborn son!" And he too was off and running. Still another said, "I haven't been in my shop in almost a year." One by one, the healed men were gone. Nine of them were gone; one stood alone. Those nine were never heard from again. They got up . . . they got out . . . but they failed to get back.

The man who stood alone in the road also had a family and a business. But something was more pressing: he felt compelled to get back to Jesus, his Healer. Perhaps you are on a similar road today. You were in crisis, you called out to God for mercy, and you stepped out in faith. But when the blessing of His answer came, you—like the nine—did not get back to Him with gratitude. And when you didn't, you missed the moment, a very important moment.

Note that the Bible simply says, "And one of them . . . returned" (Luke 17:15). One of them! We are never told his name. He is among that vast throng of people who live beautiful lives of faithfulness and gratitude, whose devotion to God is evident in worthwhile and often anonymous acts. We do not know this leper's name, but he is shouting to us today, "Get back to Jesus! Be grateful! Give thanks! If you don't, you will miss an amazing moment with your Lord."

When the leper again stood before Jesus, our Lord asked him

three rhetorical questions designed to prompt personal reflection: "Were there not ten cleansed?" Yes! "Where are the nine?" He wasn't asking a question as much as He was making an observation. Then He asked, "Were there not any found who returned to give glory to God except this foreigner?" (vv. 17–18). An alarming number of people who have been healed and blessed by Jesus may find themselves in the company of the nine.

Then Jesus said to this one, "Arise, go your way. Your faith has made you well" (v. 19). Consider now the important message communicated in this drama: the God of the universe wants our thanks. That's why the writer of Hebrews calls us to "continually offer the sacrifice of praise to God, that is, the fruit of our lips, giving thanks to His name. But do not forget to do good and to share, for with such sacrifices God is well pleased" (Hebrews 13:15–16).

Q & A: *"Where are the nine?"* As you, having been greatly blessed by God, stand on that road, do you find yourself among the nine who rush off to attend to other personal matters? Or are you joining the one who saw the importance of first "[entering] into His gates with thanksgiving" (Psalm 100:4)? Get up: Jesus is still passing by right now. Get out: take Him at His word and stand upon His promises. And when blessings come, always make a point to get back to Him with your gratitude and thanks.

39   DID NOT OUR HEART BURN WITHIN US?

—LUKE 24:32

*F*or three years Christ's disciples had followed Him, learned from Him, and ministered with Him when suddenly this season came to an abrupt and crashing conclusion: Jesus had been viciously executed and His body thrown into the cold, damp darkness of a tomb. All His disciples had forsaken Him and fled, making their way back to their respective homes.

Two of those followers headed home to Emmaus, a village seven miles west of Jerusalem. As they began their journey, their walk toward the sunset was descriptive of their present emotions. As they walked, they said to each other, "We were hoping that it was He who was going to redeem Israel" (Luke 24:21). But they had buried that hope in the tomb of Joseph of Arimathea. Dejected and dismayed, they were walking proof that there is never power in the present when there is no hope in the future.

Then suddenly the resurrected "Jesus Himself drew near and went with them," but they "did not know Him" (vv. 15–16). After this incredible encounter, "their eyes were opened and they knew Him; and He vanished from their sight" (v. 31). And their response? "Did not our heart burn within us while He talked with us on the road and while He opened the Scriptures to us?" (v. 32).

We pride ourselves today on our brilliant minds: many know the nuances of theological truths. We pride ourselves on our benevolent hands: commendable social actions abound. But what we really need are burning hearts that only come when we listen to Him on the road.

How can we acquire this heavenly heart burn? The answer is the same for us as it was for those two men walking the road to Emmaus two millennia ago. We must listen as Jesus speaks to us in two ways—by His Spirit and through His Scriptures.

LISTEN AS JESUS SPEAKS THROUGH HIS SPIRIT

The disciples revealed that their hearts were on fire because "He talked with us along the road" (Luke 24:32). Jesus did the talking! They had poured out their own disappointment, and then they listened to Him.

Their hearts didn't burn when they talked to Him. The two were still feeling sad and dejected. Likewise, many people today talk to Jesus in prayer, and they finish as disappointed and depressed as when they began because they have one-sided conversations.

Nor did the disciples' hearts burn when they conversed about Him with each other. Our own testifying to others about Him does not result in a burning heart. Their hearts burned "when He talked with us" (v. 32). Their hearts were set on fire when they *stopped talking* and *started listening* to Him, spirit to Spirit.

There are times when we need to cease our performance, cease our petitions, even cease our praise, and simply be still and listen. We have a God who speaks to us by His Spirit.

LISTEN AS JESUS SPEAKS THROUGH THE SCRIPTURES

These two disciples' cold hearts were set on fire when Jesus talked with them and revealed the meaning of the Scriptures to them. The Bible is a sealed book until Jesus' Spirit opens it to us. Those who do not know God can gain head knowledge about Him from the Bible, but they can never gain spiritual knowledge. And there is a difference.

As they journeyed together Jesus "expounded to them in all the Scriptures the things concerning Himself" (Luke 24:27). The word *expound* suggests translating something out of a foreign language, and the Bible is like a foreign language to anyone who does not walk in the spirit of Christ. It is a miracle book with miracle messages.

Jesus began speaking to the disciples with the story of "Moses and all the Prophets" and revealed Himself through the Scriptures (v. 27). From the Pentateuch to the Prophets, Jesus preached Jesus that evening on Emmaus Road. From Moses to Malachi He spoke of how the entire Jewish Bible speaks of Him. As He taught, a shadow of the cross fell across the Old Testament. Jesus was that Ram at Abraham's altar (Genesis 22:12–14). He was that spotless Passover Lamb whose blood was spilled to bring deliverance from death and freedom from slavery (Exodus 12:22–24). He was that scarlet thread hung out of Rahab's window (Joshua 2:17–21). And the shepherd of whom David spoke about in the Psalms? Jesus was that Shepherd too. As the disciples walked and listened, they understood that Jesus was Isaiah's Suffering Servant (Isaiah 53) as well as the fourth man in the fiery furnace with Shadrach, Meshach, and Abed-Nego (Daniel 3:19–25). No wonder their hearts "burned" within them while He talked with them and revealed the Scriptures to them on that road.

The disciples' immediate response is noteworthy. They did not say, "Oh, that's nice, but if we don't hurry, we're going to be last in the cafeteria line in Emmaus." Instead, they arose "that very hour and returned to Jerusalem" to exclaim to all the others, "The Lord is risen indeed" (Luke 24:33–34). They let their *glowing* turn into *going*. With beating, burning hearts, they hurried back to Jerusalem, around the corners and down the narrow alleys, up Mount Zion, to find the other disciples and share the good news. They shared it not as an emaciated question mark, but as a bold exclamation mark: "He is risen indeed!"

One of these two Emmaus disciples is named Cleopas (v. 18). The other is left unnamed. Some have speculated it was Cleopas's wife. Others have wondered if it was Luke since this report bears the imprint of an actual eyewitness. However, I like to think that this disciple is left unnamed so that you and I can find ourselves in this picture as we walk our very own Emmaus Road. Perhaps you are walking, as these two disciples were, with hopes dashed and dreams smashed. Stop. Look. Listen to Jesus' Spirit through His Scripture. And you too just might walk away with your own heart burning within you.

Q & A: *"Did not our heart burn within us?"* Dejection, depression, discouragement, and defeat are the experience of too many of us today. Like the two disciples, many of us have buried our own hopes. But hear this very good news: Jesus is walking with us on the road right now. And if our hearts aren't burning, perhaps it's because we simply are not listening to Him. He is still speaking now in the same way He spoke then: through His Spirit and through His Scriptures. He is risen *indeed*!

40

How Can *a* Man Be Born When He Is Old?

—JOHN 3:4

*T*his question came immediately after one of Jesus' most famous declarations: "Most assuredly, I say to you, unless one is born again, he cannot see the kingdom of God" (John 3:3). And this question was asked by a man named Nicodemus, who was the epitome of moral righteousness and theological acumen, yet he had entirely missed the point of Jesus' teaching. Jesus was not speaking of a physical birth, but of a spiritual birth. He went on to say: "That which is born of the flesh is flesh, and that which is born of the Spirit is spirit. . . . 'You must be born again' " (vv. 6–7).

"Born again"—rarely has a simple phrase been more misunderstood. And rarely has the meaning of two words been such an eternal life-and-death matter. Therefore it is essential to grasp the meaning—the who, the when, and the what—of this engaging dialogue that took place in a dark alley of a silent night in the city of Jerusalem two millennia ago. Why? Because, like Nicodemus, you too "must be born again."

THE WHO IS IMPRESSIVE

Talk about an impressive resume! Nicodemus had *prestige*:

he was a Pharisee, one of the brightest of the Jewish leaders and a recognized protector of Hebrew law and heritage.
He had *position*: Nicodemus was a member of the Sanhedrin,
the highest ruling council for the Jewish people, virtually the
Jewish Supreme Court. Nicodemus had *power*: he was "a ruler
of the Jews" (v. 1). And he had *popularity*: he was regarded as
one of the most upright, righteous, and moral men in the city.

Nicodemus's very name comes from two Greek words. One
means "superior" or "conqueror." In fact, the shoe company
Nike derives its name from this Greek word. The other means
"people" or "of the people." So Nicodemus was well named:
"superior over all the people." During his lifetime, he had
gained a reputation for intellectual prowess, moral upright-
ness, and leadership par excellence. He had no equal in all of
Israel. Today, we would count Nicodemus a fine leader in any
community. He would be a citizen of which any municipality
would be proud to call its own.

Nicodemus had it all, yet he knew there must be something more to life than all of his head knowledge. After
hearing the miraculous reports about Jesus, Nicodemus
approached Him that night, humbled himself, and said to
the lowly Galilean: "Rabbi, we know that You are a teacher
come from God; for no one can do these signs that You do
unless God is with him" (v. 2).

Nicodemus was not just any common man off the streets.
He was a well-respected Jewish leader who was an authority
on giving answers. Now he was asking Jesus to answer one for
him. The "who" is impressive.

THE WHEN IS IMPORTANT

According to John, Nicodemus "came to Jesus by night" (John 3:2). He waited until darkness enveloped the city and quietness had settled like dew upon the narrow lanes. Why? We don't know exactly. Some scholars speculate that he didn't want to invite the criticism of his ecclesiastical colleagues who thought they were too sophisticated and intellectual to come themselves. Or perhaps so many people wanted an audience with him that Nicodemus was busy from sunrise to sundown. Or maybe Nicodemus desired uninterrupted time with Jesus, who, during the daylight hours, was followed by massive crowds everywhere He went. I, however, like to think that Nicodemus was so consumed with seeking truth that he simply couldn't wait until the morning, so he went at night.

Whatever the reason, one thing is certain. Underneath his long robes that night was a heart—perhaps like yours—hungry for something more. Nicodemus definitely had an abundance of head knowledge. What Nicodemus needed was what each of us needs: a new heart. And so he came and approached Jesus, hoping that in the darkness of night, he might find the light of truth.

THE WHAT IS IMPERATIVE

Wasting no time in His conversation with Nicodemus, Jesus went directly to the point: "Unless one is born again, he cannot see the kingdom of God" (John 3:3). And the brightest man, the sharpest mind, in Jerusalem, didn't understand. "How can I?" he wondered aloud. "I can't get back in my mother's womb and be born again. How can a man be born when he is old?" (v. 4, paraphrased).

Then, looking into Jesus' loving eyes and listening to His gentle yet authoritative voice, Nicodemus began to realize that this was indeed He of whom the prophets spoke. Nicodemus had spent his entire life studying, teaching, and applying the Word of God. Now, before his very eyes, was the Word Incarnate.

Jesus said to Nicodemus—and His message applies to you and me—"Do not marvel that I say to you, 'You must be born again'" (v. 7). It is not an option. It is a command, an imperative. We who desire to see and to enter the kingdom of God *must* be born again. The apostle Paul, a member of the Sanhedrin himself, later described this as being "transformed" (Romans 12:2). We get our English word *metamorphosis* from this single compound Greek word. The picture is of a caterpillar spinning a cocoon around itself and later emerging as a new creation, a beautiful butterfly. No longer doomed and destined to crawl on its belly, this butterfly can now soar above the trees. Similarly, we experience a new birth when we recognize our sin, repent of that sin, and trust in Christ alone to forgive us. Yes, we MUST be born again.

Our family now makes up an even dozen with my wife and me, our two daughters, their husbands, and the six grandchildren. And each of us celebrates two birthdays every year. On our physical birthdays we gather to celebrate the life God has given and mark another year off the calendar. But we also have a celebration at each of our spiritual birthdays to remember when we were born again. January 3 is my spiritual birthday, and although I am still not the man of God I want to be, I haven't been the same since that cold January morning when, as a seventeen-year-old, I was born again.

What about Nicodemus? Did he become a follower of Christ that night? There is ample evidence in John 19 that, indeed, he did. As Jesus' body hung in death upon the cross, two men arrived, removed the spikes from His wrists and feet, took the mocking crown of thorns from His head, lowered Him from the cross, carried His body to the tomb, prepared Him for burial, and placed His lifeless body into the tomb. One of these two men was the wealthy Joseph of Arimathea in whose tomb the body was placed. And the other man? "[It was] Nicodemus, who at first came to Jesus by night . . . Then [Nicodemus and Joseph] took the body of Jesus, and bound it in strips of linen with spices, as the custom of the Jews is to bury" (vv. 39–40). Yes, "if anyone is in Christ, he is a new creation; old things have passed away; behold, all things have become new" (2 Corinthians 5:17).

Q & A: *"How can a man be born when he is old?"* A man can't be born a second time physically, but Christ can take out your old heart and put in a brand-new one. This new birth is a spiritual birth. You MUST be born again. It is not an option but a necessity for anyone who will inherit eternal life. No one—not even a righteous Pharisee, much less a rough prostitute—is exempt from this divine call and command. The new birth is God's gift to you. Receive it. By faith, come to Jesus.

41 THERE IS *a* LAD HERE WHO HAS FIVE BARLEY LOAVES *and* TWO SMALL FISH, *but* WHAT ARE THEY AMONG SO MANY?

—JOHN 6:9

*W*e have all been there. At some time or another, we have found ourselves in a situation where demand exceeded supply, where we came up short and asked ourselves, "What's the use? What is this supply in the face of so many needs?"

Jesus' disciples found themselves looking out on the multitude of people who had gathered in Galilee. It was time to eat, and the disciples had nothing to serve. Kids were crying and stomachs were growling. Then Andrew stepped forward with a little lad and a little lunch. Andrew did quite well at first: his initial words suggested his faith. "Lord, here is a boy with a few fish sandwiches! But when you think about it, what are they among so many?" Andrew was about to find out how little can become much when God gets involved.

My undergraduate degree is in business administration, and I shall never forget my very first college economics course. My professor went to the blackboard (yes, this was a few years ago) and wrote down a little formula he called the law of supply and demand. Then he turned to us and declared that it would be the foundation for everything we did in class the rest of the semester. It is a simple principle: When demand exceeds supply, prices go up. When supply exceeds demand, prices go down.

Now, what does this law of supply and demand have to do with our Lord feeding thousands of people on a Galilean hillside? Jesus was all about the law of supply and demand. Without Christ factored into life's narrative, demand will exceed supply. The people had a need for which there was no apparent supply. So their cry was "Not enough!" But when Christ got involved in the equation and multiplied the loaves and fish, supply exceeded demand (the disciples took up several baskets of leftovers). Now the crowd's cry was "More than enough!"

WITHOUT CHRIST, DEMAND EXCEEDS SUPPLY, AND THE CRY IS "NOT ENOUGH!"

Picture thousands of people away from home and hungry. There was a very large demand for which there was no apparent supply. At first, no one looked to Jesus for help. They simply threw up their hands in desperation. Phillip came upon the scene and immediately thought about how much it would cost to buy bread for that big a crowd. His first thought was the cost, not the Christ. This is always the way it is when we don't factor Christ into the equation of our life. Those who try to fill the void of life with money never have enough. How much is enough? Just a little more. How much recognition is enough for some people? Just another pat on the back. Just another round of applause. Just a little more. Why? Because the void of life on our own is so large, only Christ can fill it.

When Andrew stepped forward and said, "A lad here has five barley loaves and two small fish," it was a good enough start, but he continued with "*but* what are they among so many?" (John 6:9, emphasis added). Give him an *F*. He flunked. Andrew became part of the problem instead of the solution. Our Lord was testing him (v. 6), hoping he would say, "Lord, I don't know what to do, but I know this is no problem for You. I saw You turn water into wine. I know You can do anything." But Andrew was thinking like many of us and not factoring Christ into life's equation.

Without Christ, demand always exceeds supply, and our cry is "Not enough." It may be that you have a need today for which there is no apparent supply. Perhaps the need is physical, emotional, material, or spiritual. Little can become much when you allow Christ to get involved.

WITH CHRIST, SUPPLY EXCEEDS DEMAND, AND THE CRY IS "MORE THAN ENOUGH!"

We all know the story well. Jesus took the bread and fish, gave thanks, then miraculously multiplied it to feed the entire crowd. After everyone had eaten, the disciples picked up the leftovers and filled a dozen baskets. Yes, more than enough!

How did it happen? The boy gave. He could have clutched his little brown lunch bag and kept it to himself. But he didn't. The boy planted a seed that day. He gave. And he gave all. He could have given one loaf and one fish, but he gave all he had.

That exchange between the lad and the Lord tapped the eternal resources of heaven and moved them into the bankrupt affairs of men.

But that is still not the entire story. After the people had eaten their fill, they gave back the excess. As the boy's lunch illustrates, we never give the Lord anything and see it wasted. Remember, it is not the size of your lunch that matters, but whether you are willing to factor Christ into the equation of your life and let Him do what only He can. Because little is much when He is involved.

Q & A: "*What are they among so many?*" Not much at all if you only look with human eyes. But Christ has bigger and better plans. The thought that strikes me most in this story is that this lad left home that morning with the potential to feed thousands of people with his little lunch—and he didn't even know it. It may be that you who are reading these words right now have incredible potential . . . and don't even realize it. Yes, little is much when you factor Christ into the equation of your life.

42   DO YOU BELIEVE THIS?

*I*t was a sad and somber day in Bethany as Jesus stood in the midst of the brokenhearted family and friends at the grave of Lazarus. From His lips came an astonishing claim: "I am the resurrection and the life. He who believes in Me, though he may die, he shall live. And whoever lives and believes in Me shall never die" (John 11:25–26). Then Jesus looked into their faces—just as He looks into our hearts—and asked life's bottom-line question: "Do you believe this?" (v. 26).

The resurrection is what sets our Lord apart from a thousand other gurus and self-proclaimed prophets who have come along through the centuries. The question, "Do you believe this?" is what drives any responsible hearer to either accept or reject the Christian faith.

Since we obviously have no audio recordings or videos of our Lord's words, I have often wondered what words He emphasized in statements He made and questions He asked. Here in Bethany did He ask, "Do *you* believe this?" After all, it is a personal matter. Or did He ask, "Do you *believe* this?" It is certainly a very pointed question. Or did He ask, "Do you believe *this*?" His question is also precise. Confronted with this bottom-line question of life, may you answer with

Martha, "Yes, Lord, I believe that You are the Christ, the Son of God, who is to come into the world" (v. 27).

LIFE'S BOTTOM-LINE QUESTION IS PERSONAL

Perhaps Jesus emphasized the *you* in order to drive home the fact that one's salvation is a very personal and individual matter: "Do *you* believe this?" When it comes to saving faith in the finished work of Christ, what matters is not what my mother or father, husband or wife, or anyone else believes. It is a personal matter. I have, however, known some who pinned all their hopes of eternal life on someone else's faith as though they might eventually benefit by some sort of spiritual osmosis. The real question is, "Do *you* believe this?" It is intensely personal.

One of the intrigues of our modern gnostic culture is the number of people captivated by certain books and movies that question the veracity of the Gospel accounts. Some people refuse to believe Jesus is the Son of God. What about you? Do you really want to believe that His death was, in essence, an unnecessary event and not voluntarily and vicariously experienced for you personally? Or that His resurrection should be relegated to some ancient shelf of obscurity along with other ancient myths and fables?

The question is personal. "Do *you* believe this?"

LIFE'S BOTTOM-LINE QUESTION IS POINTED

It could be that when Jesus asked this question in the Bethany cemetery, He emphasized the word *believe* and asked it thus: "Do you *believe* this?" He was not asking His hearers if they were giving intellectual assent to His claims. He wanted to know if they would actually put their total trust and faith in His words.

It is one thing to know the gospel story intellectually. It is one thing to attempt to conform ourselves to the resurrection by trying to take up a new set of moral standards externally. It is even one thing to reason and argue in the defense of the gospel. But the real issue for Jesus was—and is—one of faith: "Do you *believe* this?" Life's bottom-line question is not only personal but pointed as well.

LIFE'S BOTTOM-LINE QUESTION IS PRECISE

Now we come to the heart of the issue. True faith must rest on objective truth and fact. It may well be that Jesus placed emphasis on the last word in the question: "Do you believe *this*?" Do we believe what? Note the context. Jesus asked this question on the direct heels of an amazing claim: "I am the resurrection and the life. He who believes in Me, though he may die, he shall live. And whoever lives and believes in Me shall never die! Do you believe *this*?" (John 11:25–26, empahsis added).

Do you believe *this*—Jesus' claim of *deity*? "I am the resurrection and the life." Using the words "I am" captured the attention of those around Him. John's gospel records an "I am" statement by Jesus seven times. We first hear God use this "I am" statement way back in Exodus 3:13–14 when Moses asked the voice from the burning bush to reveal His name. God simply instructed Moses to tell the children of Israel, "I AM has sent me to you." When Jesus said, "I am," all those listening recognized it to be an affirmation of His deity.

The most fundamental belief of the Christian faith is that Jesus of Nazareth is God Himself. This is why the apostle Paul would say, "He is the image of the invisible God. . . . All things were created through Him and for Him" (Colossians 1:15–16). It was this faith in His deity that would later lead Paul, the disciples, and so many early believers to their own martyrs' deaths.

Do you believe *this*—His claim about *death*? Jesus said, "Though he may die"(John 11:25), meaning "though *you* may die!" Many live in total denial of this coming appointment. One of life's greatest facts is that you are going to die. Recently, I was looking through a stack of pictures from over a decade ago. I was stunned. My hair was darker. My face looked so much younger. It dawned on me that this body of mine has death in it. I am decaying right before my eyes. Some people opt for plastic surgery, have liposuction, or regularly take handfuls of vitamins and supplements. But none of that can stop the fact that we are marching toward death, our final enemy.

Death is humankind's common denominator. Just look at the obituary section of your newspaper. On the society page you will read of only one class of people. In the sports section you will read only of those who are gifted in athletics. In the business section, only those who are noteworthy are featured. But on the obituary page, everyone is listed side by side, in simple, cold, alphabetical order. Death knocks on the door of the wealthiest billionaire and the poorest of peasants and sends them both to stand before the Judge of the universe. No wonder Amos thundered out the warning, "Prepare to meet your God" (Amos 4:12).

Do you believe *this*?—Jesus' claim about *destiny*? "Though he may die . . . he shall live" (John 11:25). What Jesus means is, the body may die, but not the spirit. There is a part of you that will live on as long as God lives, which is forever. Do you believe His claim that death is not the end; that even though our bodies will one day die, we will still live in spirit? There is another life that is more than a million times longer than this one: it is an eternity we will spend . . . with Him. Do you believe *this*? Do you believe Jesus' claim about His deity and our own death and destiny?

There are a lot of big questions in life. Most of them will be asked when we are young adults, without the wisdom and perspective that come with everyday life experience: "Where will I attend college? What will be my chosen life profession? With whom will I spend my life?" But there is only one big question in death, and it is: "Do you believe this?" You can settle the answer now, once and for all, by joining Martha in her response: "Yes, Lord, I believe that You are the Christ, the Son of God" (John 11:27).

$Q \& A$: *"Do you believe this?"* You are the only one who can answer this bottom-line question of life because it is intensely personal: "Do *you* believe this?" Yet the question is also pointed: "Do you *believe* this?" Without faith it is impossible to please God. And this question Jesus asked is precise: "Do you believe *this*?" As for me, thankfully, I addressed this question long ago by trusting in Jesus and declaring, "Yes, Lord, I believe that You are the Christ, the Son of God."

43

DO YOU LOVE ME
MORE THAN THESE?

—JOHN 21:15

*W*hat do you do when you've blown it?

Simon Peter had been so proud when he boasted that he would never betray the Lord, but Peter's pride inevitably turned to shame: he did betray Jesus. And on the very night Jesus needed him the most. For several days Peter's disappointment in himself had been playing over and over in his mind. How he wished he could go back in time!

So what do you do when you've failed? Do you find something to occupy yourself, to take your mind off your failure? That's what Peter and a half dozen other disciples who were in the same situation did—they went fishing. All night they fished . . . with absolutely zero success. At morning light they heard a familiar voice from the nearby shore: "Cast the net on the right of the boat, and you will find some" (John 21:6). They did—and they did! Peter, always the impulsive one, didn't wait for the others. He plunged into the sea, swam to shore, and saw the crucified and risen Lord . . . alive! Together they had breakfast on the beach. Jesus looked at him and asked, "Simon, son of Jonah, do you love Me more than these?" (v. 15).

For Simon Peter, this day marked a new beginning. Coming to grips with this question enabled him to realize his potential, which he had lost sight of after his devastating failure, after he had denied knowing his Savior. This question enabled Peter to recognize anew his purpose and to realign his priorities. A fresh encounter with the Lord Jesus will bring a new beginning to any of us who come face-to-face with the question, "Do *you* love Me more than these?" It is never too late for a new beginning. Just ask Simon Peter.

FRESH ENCOUNTERS ENABLE US TO REALIZE OUR POTENTIAL

When Peter arrived on shore, Jesus referred to him as "Simon," not Peter, not Simon Peter. Just Simon—and this is significant. Simon was his old name. When our Lord first encountered him three years earlier, Jesus said, "You are Simon the son of Jonah. You shall be called Cephas (which is translated, A Stone)" (John 1:42). Jesus used a play on words. *Simon* means a small pebble; *Cephas* means a large rock or boulder. Jesus looked at Simon Peter not for who he was then, but for who he could become: a solid rock. Jesus clearly saw the potential in Peter's life.

After this first encounter, Jesus never referred to him as Simon again—until this breakfast on the beach. And why did Jesus choose that name at this time? Because His impetuous disciple had been living in his old nature. When the test came in Caiaphas's courtyard after Jesus' arrest, Peter acted as he had before he met the Lord. Peter lied. He cursed. He denied. Now when he heard Jesus refer to him as "Simon," that name was like an arrow piercing his heart. That name reminded Peter of the potential Jesus had seen in him, the potential He now wanted to recover. Fresh encounters with the living Christ will do this for us. Meeting Jesus anew will not simply cause us to sense our shortcomings, but will also inspire us to reach the potential He still sees in us.

FRESH ENCOUNTERS ENABLE US TO RECOGNIZE OUR PURPOSE

The bottom line for Peter—and for us—is whether we truly love the Lord Jesus. He still asks us today, "Do you love *Me*?" After all, as Jesus stated in the Great Commandment, loving the Lord Jesus is our primary purpose in life (Matthew 22:37–38).

But what strikes me about this encounter between the Lord and His sometimes follower is not just what Jesus said, but what He *didn't* say. He didn't say to Peter, "Some friend you turned out to be. I had you figured all wrong. You are just all talk. You failed. You let Me down after boasting so often and so loudly about how faithful you would be at the crisis hour." No, Jesus looked at Peter and simply asked, "Do you love Me?" Three times in rapid succession, He asked the same question. He was giving Peter three opportunities to counter his three denials that he knew Jesus, statements he had proclaimed before the rooster crowed at dawn a few days earlier.

Jesus' question to Peter is also the bottom-line question for us. It is not whether we love one another or love the lost and lonely. It is "Do you love *Me*?" Loving Jesus is our primary purpose, and doing so affects all other issues in life for our good and His glory. Fresh encounters with the living Christ will enable us not simply to realize the potential that is locked within us, but also to recognize afresh and anew our primary purpose in life.

FRESH ENCOUNTERS ENABLE US TO REALIGN OUR PRIORITIES

Then, going a step further, Jesus qualified His question to Peter as well as to us: "Do you love Me more than these?" These what? These who? Peter was surrounded by his best friends and fishing buddies. They traveled together, ate together, laughed together, wept together. Simon Peter was always the life of the party. He was a born leader, a classic type A personality. Could "these" mean more than these other people? Was Jesus asking Peter, "Do you love Me more than you love your friends and partners in ministry?" Also, Peter was back near his hometown in Galilee where everything was so familiar—the landscape, the people. Could Jesus mean "Do you love Me more than you love the comforts of your sentimental surroundings?" Nearby were the boats, the nets, the fishing business he had known all his life. Could Jesus mean "Do you love Me more than you love your possessions"? By asking Peter, "Do you love Me more than these?" Jesus was having Peter zero in on his own priorities.

When, as believers, we have our priorities properly aligned and we love the Lord Jesus more than we love life itself, it is amazing how other areas of life seem to fall into place.

Now we see one of the most beautiful manifestations ever of our Lord's tenderness and grace. Jesus asked Peter these three questions, which on the surface seem simply the same question asked three times: "Do you love Me? . . . Do you love Me? . . . Do you love Me?" (John 21:15–17). But let's look more closely. First, remember that John recorded this encounter not in English, but in the universal written language of his day, Koine Greek. The Greek language is much more expressive about love than the English vernacular. No matter what the reference to love in the original language may imply, we use the same word to say, "I love my wife. I love my dog. I love Mexican food." The Greeks, however, had three words that we translate *love*. One was the highest level of love, *agape*— God's love that is sacrificial and sanctifying, always seeking the other's highest good above our own. The next level of love in Greek was *philos* and referred to affection, to a brotherly type of love. Think about Philadelphia and its nickname, "The City of Brotherly Love." Finally, the Greeks used *eros* (think "erotic") to refer to the lowest level of love, to a merely physical attraction. Now we're ready to look again at Jesus' question.

When Jesus asked Peter, "Do you love Me?" in verse 15, Jesus used the word *agape*. That is, "Peter, do you love Me with this godly, sacrificial, unconditional kind of love?" Peter used a different word for love in his answer: "Yes, Lord; You know that I love You" (v. 16). But Peter used *philos*, referring to this brotherly fondness as if he was very aware of his limited ability to love. Aware of his failure to love, Peter was no longer boasting.

Again, Jesus inquired about Peter's love for Him in verse 16, and again Jesus used *agape* to refer to this highest level of love. Now, grieved in his heart, Peter still could not bring himself to claim as he had in the past that he could love with *agape* love. Continuing to be open and honest, Peter again used the word *philos*. Peter loved the Lord, but Peter knew his limitations: Peter knew he wasn't able to love the way Jesus loves.

Finally, Jesus asked Peter a third time, "Do you love Me?" (v. 17). But this time He came down to Peter's level and used the word *philos*: "Peter, as best you can, here and now, do you love Me?" This is amazing condescension. And Peter replied, "Lord, You know all things. You know I love you!"

New beginnings are not automatic. They involve the true confession of our shortcomings and a realignment of our priorities. Consider the fruit of those two steps in Peter's life: Peter went away from this encounter to become the Spirit-filled preacher of Pentecost and the undisputed leader of the Jerusalem church. It is never too late for a new beginning! And a new beginning will do three things for you, just as it did for Peter. A new beginning will enable you to realize your potential, recognize your purpose, and realign your priorities.

Our Lord is still waiting on the shore for you . . . and me.

Q & A: *"Do you love Me more than these?"* Look around you this week and then join Peter in answering, "Yes, Lord, You know all things. You know I love You . . . You know I love You more than I love these." Jesus sees you now just as He saw Simon Peter, not for who you are, but for who you can become. So with Jesus' help, realize your potential, recognize your primary purpose in life, and realign your priorities. When you do, you will hear—as Peter did—those two simple and life-changing words, "Follow Me" (John 21:19).

44   WHAT SHALL WE DO?

—ACTS 2:37

*O*ften in the Christian experience, it is not that we don't want to do the right thing, we simply don't know what the right thing is to do.

This Acts 2:37 question came in response to Peter's proclamation of the gospel of Jesus Christ on the day when Pentecost marked the coming of the Holy Spirit. Upon hearing of the death, burial, and resurrection of Jesus, people felt convicted of their sins, their "hearts were cut," and they cried out, "What shall we do?" Peter's pointed yet poignant one-word response was "Repent" (v. 38). Now if there was ever a lost word in our twenty-first-century Christian vocabulary and the modern era of positive preaching, *repentance* is the forgotten word!

Although too often relegated to a dusty shelf today, repentance was the central theme of our Lord's message. Jesus *commenced* His ministry with this theme: "From that time Jesus began to preach, and to say, 'Repent, for the kingdom of heaven is at hand'" (Matthew 4:17). Jesus *continued* to share this message in his ministry: "I tell you . . . unless you repent you will all likewise perish" (Luke 13:3). And Jesus *concluded* His ministry with that same truth: "Thus it is written, and thus it was necessary for the Christ to suffer and to rise from the dead the third day, and that repentance and remission of sins should be preached in His name to all nations, beginning at Jerusalem" (Luke 24:46–47).

Repentance is among the most misunderstood and, I daresay, most ignored disciplines of the Christian life. Ask multiple people to define it, and you will get multiple answers.

REPENTANCE IS NOT REMORSE

Repentance is not simply being sorry that we have sinned—or that we've been caught in our sin. Remorse—which *is* sorrow for one's sin—often leads to repentance, but repentance is much more than that. Remember the rich young ruler? He went to Jesus, but when he heard of the demands of discipleship, he "went away sorrowful" (Matthew 19:22). This young man was remorseful, but he wasn't willing to repent. One of the reasons so many people flounder in their faith is due to the fact that they have tried to substitute remorse for repentance. It is not enough simply to be sorry for our sin or troubled by our transgressions.

REPENTANCE IS NOT REGRET

Repentance is also not merely wishing the deed had never happened and regretting it. Pontius Pilate, the Roman governor who betrayed our Lord, took the basin of water and attempted to wash his hands of his evil deed: he regretted that it had happened, but he didn't repent. Many people today substitute regret for repentance and, by doing so, tragically fool themselves about where they stand with the Lord.

REPENTANCE IS NOT RESOLVE

All of us have made New Year's resolutions. Most of us have resolved at one time or another to, for instance, strive to live by a new set of moral standards. We want to live life on a higher plane, but we often fail to do so. One reason is because we are attempting to substitute our own resolve for genuine repentance.

REPENTANCE IS NOT REFORM

Repentance is not simply my turning over a new leaf and trying hard to reform my ways. Judas Iscariot betrayed our Lord for thirty pieces of silver, but he later took the money back to the temple and threw it at those who had paid the bribe. Judas reformed his ways to the degree that he returned the blood money, but unfortunately he didn't repent.

No remorse, resolve, regret, nor reformation will substitute for repentance. So, "What shall we do?" What, then, *is* repentance? Is it possible to repent without even knowing how to define it? My life was radically transformed when, as a teenager, I invited Christ to come into my heart, but it was months afterwards before I ever heard the word *repentance*. Still, I know that I repented—and that I did so instantaneously. The clear evidence was that I began to hate what I used to love and love what I used to hate. I experienced a change of mind . . . which changed my will or volition . . . which ultimately changed my actions.

The Greek word translated "repent" simply means to

change one's mind. This genuine change of mind is always evidenced in three ways. First comes the new *attitude.* That is, repentance begins intellectually with a change of mind. After this occurs, we experience a change of heart, a change of *affections.* A change in our will, our volition, will follow, and that is evident in a change of *action.* As naturally as water running downhill, my will changes, and that change will result in a change in my actions.

If you need a perfect biblical illustration of genuine repentance, look no further than the story of the prodigal son in Luke 15. Here is a rebellious young man who had left home for the bright lights of the big city and ended up in a pig pen feeding hogs. There, he had a change of *attitude.* The gospel writer put it this way: "he came to himself" (v. 17). He changed his mind. Then what happened? He had a change of *affection.* He said, "I will arise and go to my father and say . . . 'I am no longer worthy to be called your son'" (vv. 18–19). His heart was changed. Then, his *action* followed. "He arose" and went home (v. 20).

I love the way Paul framed it in the Roman epistle: "The goodness of God leads you to repentance" (Romans 2:4). When our daughters were young we used to vacation in the Smoky Mountains. On one occasion we rented an old farmhouse on the side of a mountain. It was a beautiful spot but a bit scary for two little city girls. The first night happened to be one of those pitch-dark nights. As James Weldon Johnson put it in *God's Trombones,* it was "blacker than a hundred midnights down in a cypress swamp." I was awakened in the middle of the night by the cries of our little seven-year-old. I bounded up the stairs to find her standing there in the darkness, disoriented and scared. Taking her by the hand, I led her safely down the stairs into our own bed where she soundly slept the rest of the night away.

And so our dear heavenly Father finds us in the dark, disoriented, and takes us by the hand, and by His own goodness and kindness, "leads us to repentance."

Jesus said it best: "Unless you repent you will all likewise perish" (Luke 13:3). What difference does it make if you drive the most luxurious car money can buy, eat vitamin-enriched foods, sleep on a name-brand mattress, live in a mansion behind iron gates, are placed in a multi-thousand dollar mahogany casket, and buried in a cemetery as beautiful as a botanical garden—and rise up in judgment to meet a God you do not know? What shall we do? Change your mind and your heart will follow, and then your actions will also.

Q & A : "*What shall we do?*" It is not enough to simply know "about" Christ without knowing Him personally in the free pardoning of our sins. And this is only possible by personal repentance. What shall we do? The instructions are straightforward and direct: *repent, for the kingdom of heaven is at hand!*

45

LORD, WHAT DO YOU WANT ME *to* DO?

—ACTS 9:6

September 11, 2001, is a date like December 7, 1941—one that will live on in infamy. America was suddenly awakened to the reality that terrorism was not simply confined to the Middle East. Certainly, twenty-first-century terrorism is nothing new to that part of the world. One of the cruelest terrorist attacks of the first century took center stage in Acts, chapter 9. The man was en route from Jerusalem to Damascus, and his goal was clear: stamp out a Christian uprising there. In Acts 8 his terrorist cell, operating out of Jerusalem, had successfully eliminated Stephen, the first Christian martyr. The traveler was engaged in a systematic attempt to use intimidation and murder to crush this new and expanding church. This traveler—named Saul—was the master terrorist of his day, and like today's terrorists, his evil acts were in the name of religion.

But something happened that transformed him. "Suddenly a light shone round him from heaven. Then he fell to the ground, and heard a voice saying to him, 'Saul, Saul, why are you persecuting Me?' And he said, 'Who are You, Lord?'" (Acts 9:3–5). The risen Christ revealed Himself to Saul who, "trembling and astonished," asked, "Lord, what do You want me to do?" (v. 6). You may know the story: Saul was gloriously converted to faith in Christ. Saul of Tarsus miraculously became the apostle Paul, the passionate preacher who, from his own pen, gave us almost half of our New Testament. Having found God's will for his life, Paul spent the rest of his days spreading the gospel message and planting churches throughout the Mediterranean world. Then, at the end, outside the city gates of Rome, he was beheaded for sharing the gospel of Christ.

Paul's question in Acts 9:6 is the question every one of us should ask: "Lord, what do You want me to do?" Each of us is unique: no one has a thumbprint like yours; no one has DNA like yours. No wonder, then, God has a job for you to do that no one else can do quite like you can. Paul never stopped asking this question. Too many of God's people, however, take the opposite approach and each morning say, "Lord, here are my orders for today: bless me, take care of my family, meet this need for me, and straighten out that other person." Isn't it time for a new day to dawn when we start asking, "Lord, what do *You* want *me* to do today?"

There is a purpose for your life, accompanied by a divine plan, and it existed even before you took your first breath. Through Jeremiah God frames it, "Before I formed you in the womb I knew you; before you were born I sanctified you; I ordained you a prophet to the nations" (Jeremiah 1:5). Think about that. Like both Paul and Jeremiah, you have a God-given purpose and role in His kingdom that was established even before you were born. God knew you, and He set you apart from all others. He gave you a job that no one can do quite like you can. Discovering this amazing truth brings the question, "Lord, what do You want me to do?" into clearer focus. Just think about your testimony as a Christ-follower.

THE LORD KNEW ME

What an awesome and profound thought, that God says to you and me, "Before I formed you in the womb I knew you" (Jeremiah 1:5). Before your own parents knew you, before I was even conceived, God knew you and me! He didn't merely know we were in the womb. There is nothing remarkable about that. Anyone could conclude that along the way of a mother's pregnancy. But God knew me and God knew you *before* either of us were even formed in our mothers' wombs.

You are not an accident. There is a specific, tailor-made design for your life. He has a purpose and a plan for you. Think of it. Before you were born, God knew you.

THE LORD SET ME APART

God continues to speak through the words of His prophet Jeremiah and says, "Before you were born I sanctified you" (Jeremiah 1:5). The word *sanctified* means that you are separated, set apart, treated as holy. Nothing you did or didn't do brought this sanctification about. He set you apart from all others, and considers you sacred.

This is another awesome thought. God also set apart a day of the week, the Sabbath, to be different from all the rest just as He set apart a tenth of our income as holy and separate from the rest. He did the same with you. God not only knew you but He set you apart from all others. Thus, to use your life for any other reason than to primarily glorify Him would be a sacrilege. You are indescribably special to Him. Tragically, however, too many people live their entire lives without ever realizing this truth.

THE LORD GAVE ME A JOB

To Jeremiah, God said, "I ordained you a prophet to the nations" (Jeremiah 1:5). God has also "ordained" you for a special task for which He has uniquely gifted you. This word means "to assign; to designate." This same word is used to describe how God "set [the stars] in the firmament" (Genesis 1:17). Each one of the millions of stars has its own appointed place set by God, and they all move in clocklike precision. Just as God has set and assigned each star in the heavens, He has assigned you a job that no one can do quite like you can. Realize that true success in life comes with knowing God's will for your life . . . and doing it.

Let me illustrate this point with a truth about me that my wife can attest to: I have never been known for my handyman skills. When we moved our youngest daughter into her college dorm, I was assigned the task of assembling a small pedestal table. Only four screws were involved, so how hard could it be? After examining the situation I realized right away that each of the screws were of the Phillips variety with a little grooved cross in them; I needed a Phillips screwdriver. But in my impatience, I quickly grabbed a kitchen knife that was close by, pressed it into the screw, and worked hard to turn it down tight, but with little success. Later, I found Susie's little toolbox, got the Phillips screwdriver from it, and it fit those little grooves perfectly. It felt so satisfying to turn the screw tight. And I felt pretty good about myself in the process. What was the difference? The screwdriver was doing exactly what it was made to do! If you are trying really hard at a task but not succeeding, maybe you aren't doing exactly what God intended for you all along, what He fashioned and formed you to do. Find out what that purpose is, because in doing it will come satisfaction. Simply put, it will feel right.

Follow Paul's example from the Damascus Road. Ask, "Lord, what do You want me to do?" Stop going through life trying to tighten a Phillips screw with a kitchen knife. It will never work right. Instead, ask God to show you the job He has for you to do that no one can do like you. There is a divine purpose for you . . . there is a plan for you . . . and it was in place even before you were born!

$Q \, \& \, A$: *"Lord, what do You want me to do?"* Are you following the will of God in your life? Are you willing to be what He wants you to be and to do what He wants you to do? If not, are you willing to be made willing? Success and fulfillment in life is in finding the answer to this question for yourself. It is the ability to find God's plan for you . . . and then do it!

46   WHAT MUST I DO *to* BE SAVED?

—ACTS 16:30

*W*e come now to what is arguably the most pointed question in the entire Bible: "What must I do to be saved?" A jailer in the ancient city of Philippi asked his prisoners, Paul and Silas, this question in the midnight hour. Hours earlier this same jailer had beaten them, put them inside a prison cell, and fastened their feet in iron stocks. Why was the jailer now asking the two prisoners about spiritual matters? To fully appreciate the motivation behind this question we must view it in the context in which it was asked.

It was in the midnight hour. The jailer had securely locked Paul and Silas in the "inner prison" (Acts 16:24)—they had bloody, beaten backs and their feet were secured in iron stocks, but their voices were "praying and singing hymns to God" (v. 25). Then suddenly God went into action. He sent an earthquake that not only shook the foundation of the prison, but opened the prison doors and loosed the prisoners' chains. Knowing that punishment for letting the prisoners escape would be his death, the jailer drew his sword to do the deed himself when he saw that the prisoners had not escaped. Amazed, the jailer "fell down trembling before Paul and Silas" and asked, "Sirs, what must I do to be saved?" Their

236

reply was immediate: "Believe on the Lord Jesus Christ, and you will be saved, you and your household" (Acts 16:29–31).

When darkness sets into our lives, when the midnight hour comes, we often feel like giving up—we certainly don't feel like singing a song in the night! But singing praises has a hugely liberating effect on three relationships in life. First, praise affects our inward expression—our relationship with ourselves. Second is our upward expression—our relationship with God. And third, our outward expression—our relationship with others. A song in the night engages all three relationships and often leads others to inquire about what enables us to live in such victory.

A SONG IN THE NIGHT WILL ALTER OUR PERSPECTIVE

As to the inward expression, singing a song in the night will change our perspective, improve our attitude, and get the attention of others. That was true for Paul and Silas as well. Nothing seemed to be going right for them. They had been arrested. Their backs were sore and bleeding. Their bodies ached. It would have been easy for Paul and Silas to have asked the question of Gideon, "If the LORD is with us, why then has all this happened to us?" (Judges 6:13). But instead, they chose to sing a song of praise, and it altered their perspective. Jesus had given Paul and Silas what the prophet Isaiah had foretold: "the garment of praise for the spirit of heaviness" (Isaiah 61:3). Often when things are not going our way, our own attitude can make a tough situation even more difficult. An accurate perspective is vital, especially when it is midnight in our soul. Giving thanks to God and singing His praise will alter our perspective as the Lord's light of hope breaks through.

A SONG IN THE NIGHT WILL ACTIVATE OUR POWER

God always hears His people when we sing a song in the night. He often responds with the blessing of peace and comfort. But in Acts 16, His response was more dramatic: "Suddenly"— and I love that word—"there was a great earthquake . . . and immediately"—another good word—"all the doors were opened and everyone's chains were loosed" (v. 26).

In Psalm 22, David wrote that God is "enthroned in the praises of Israel" (v. 3). In other words, God inhabits the praises of His people. Our praise is where God is at home! This is where He gets comfortable and settles in. And so, in the darkness of their prison cell, Paul and Silas sang a song in the night, and God responded with a remarkable demonstration of His power.

When difficulties come knocking on our door, when we find ourselves in our own prison at midnight, we can too easily assume the martyr's role and begin to get comfortable in the cell of self-pity. Resist that! Instead, sing a song in the night. It will alter your own perspective, and it will activate the power of God in your behalf to endure. There is power in praise.

A SONG IN THE NIGHT WILL ALLEVIATE
OUR PREJUDICES

Talk about prejudices in the outward expression of relationships! People in Macedonia thought none too highly of Jews, and then when Paul and Silas began preaching the gospel message—which they deemed too controversial for their own tastes—the Macedonians' prejudice increased. But when Paul and Silas sang a song in the night, they became a blessing to others. The very jailer who had whipped those stripes in their backs was now drawn to them, curious about what made them different, interested in their message.

When we are in our own midnight hour and we begin to praise our God in the midst of it, we often catch the attention of people around us who are watching to see how we react. The world looks on, as this jailer did, and concludes that it wants what we have.

Picture the jailer as he knelt, trembling, before Paul and Silas and asked, "Sirs, what must I do to be saved?" The jailer felt convicted by God's Spirit. Shaking and kneeling, he wondered what he had to *do* to be saved. But the jailer could not *do* anything. It had already been *done*: Christ's death on the cross is what saves. So when the jailer asked about how to be saved, the disciples' immediate reply was "Believe!" Put your trust in Christ alone, they said, "and you will be saved!" (Acts 16:31). The jailer learned late that night that salvation is not spelled D-O, but D-O-N-E!

A beautiful thing happens before our story ends: the jailer

"took them the same hour of the night and washed their stripes" (Acts 16:33). Only the gospel can change a man's heart like that. The jailer was now gently washing and seeking to soothe the very stripes on their backs from the beating he himself had earlier administered. What a testimony to the fact that "if anyone is in Christ, he is a new creation; old things have passed away; behold, all things have become new" (2 Corinthians 5:17).

Q & A: *"What must I do to be saved?"* The pointed answer is the same today: "Believe on the Lord Jesus Christ, and you will be saved" (Acts 16:31). It is as easy as ABC: **A**dmit your sin and come to Christ in true humility and need just as this jailer did. **B**elieve that Jesus is the resurrected Son of God and trust that He alone can save you from the deadly consequences of your sin. After all, it is "by grace you have been saved through faith, and that not of yourselves; it is the gift of God, not of works, lest anyone should boast" (Ephesians 2:8–9). **C**onfess your faith, because "if you confess with your mouth the Lord Jesus and believe in your heart that God has raised Him from the dead, you will be saved" (Romans 10:9). Yes, salvation is spelled D-O-N-E. Your part is to believe!

47

IF GOD IS *for* US, WHO CAN BE AGAINST US?

—ROMANS 8:31

*I*t has often been said, and with good reason, that when it comes to the Bible, a text without a context becomes simply a pretext, or presumption. In Romans 8:31 the question, "If God is for us, who can be against us?" is preceded by the question, "What then shall we say to these things?" Thus, before we can accurately answer the question of our chapter, we must address what "these things" are that Paul mentions.

"What then can we say to these things?" What things? The wonderful news just preceding Romans 8:28–30 is that we have a God who is watching over us and who is also at work for our good. Paul prefaced the questions of verse 31 by saying:

> We know that all things work together for good to those who love God, to those who are the called according to His purpose. For whom He foreknew, He also predestined to be conformed to the image of His Son, that He might be the firstborn among many brethren. Moreover whom He predestined, these He also called; whom He called, these He also justified; and whom He justified, these He also glorified (vv. 28–30).

Then the apostle asked, "What then shall we say to these things?"—to these amazing truths? And he answered with another question: "If God be for us, who can be against us?" The obvious answer? It doesn't matter who may be against us when almighty God Himself is for us, for He is always at work watching over us and providing for us.

GOD IS WATCHING OVER US

We find this wonderful truth wrapped in the package of one of the most quoted verses in all the Bible: "And we know that all things work together for good to those who love God, to those who are the called according to His purpose" (Romans 8:28). I like to think of this as the secret of God's forever family.

This family secret is *confidential*: "We know." The lost world has no concept that God is watching over us and working on our behalf, but His followers do. We do not wish, or think, or hope. We *know* that He is. Confront the existentialist today who sees and says there is no purpose in events that are happening in life. We say, "Oh, there is definitely a purpose, but it's confidential. Only those who love Him can unlock this truth. It's a family secret."

Our family secret is also *constructive*. Paul said, "Things work together for good." I look back over my life, and I remember issues that came my way that, at the time, I thought were so detrimental. Now I clearly see that God allowed them for a greater purpose. In retrospect I see that God indeed worked them together for my own good, to make me more like His Son.

This truth about God's good work is also *comprehensive.* Note that the verse says "*all* things." Can I believe this? Had Paul said "some things" or "many things" or even "most things" are working to my good, it would be more palatable. But "all things"? Yes, even unfair things—like Joseph being held in an Egyptian jail. Difficult things? Yes, ask those early Jerusalem believers who had to leave their homes and jobs and were dispersed over the world, resulting in the spread of the gospel. "All things"—not necessarily each as an isolated event, but when woven together by God in the tapestry of the cross in our lives—"work together for good."

Finally, our family secret is *conditional.* It is given to those of us who are "called according to His purpose." Is the purpose of God—His will for your life—being accomplished in you? Are you cooperating, seeking to walk according to His guidance, and living confidently as a child of the King?

GOD IS WORKING FOR US

Paul continued with what, in essence, is a chain of five strong and interdependent links. Take away any link in the chain, and it all falls apart.

The first link is the *wisdom* of God: "for whom He foreknew" (Romans 8:29). The Greek word means "to know before." We get our word *prognosis* from this ancient word. This is one of the most intimate words in the Greek language. God has known every intricate detail of my life before any of those details unfolded. You say, "I can't understand all that." Well, neither can I! But I have decided that if I could, with my finite human mind, He would really not be very big.

Next follows the *will* of God link: "whom He foreknew, He also predestined" (v. 29). Perhaps there is no word that causes others to bristle as much as the word *predestined* does. And it just might be one of the most misunderstood of all words. It comes from two Greek words meaning "before" and "horizon." In eternity past God set out some boundaries *before* the *horizon*. Predestination doesn't have anything to do with people; it has everything to do with purposes. In the text, Paul indicated we are "predestined"—to what?—"to be conformed to the image of His Son." Election deals with people. But predestination deals with God's purposes, with His will for us.

Firmly attached to these links of God's wisdom and will is the *way* of God: "whom He predestined, these He also called" (v. 30). God "issued a summons" to us in two calls. The outward call we hear from the preacher or a teacher or when we read a challenging book. But there is also the inward call from our God who is working for our benefit, speaking to our hearts, Spirit to spirit. God is working. First, God foreknows, then He predestines, and then He calls.

Next in the chain—after God's wisdom, will, and way—comes the *work* of God: "whom He called, these He also justified" (v. 30). The Greek word means "to make pure and free." It is not our own works that justify us; only the finished work of Christ on the cross makes us able to stand before our holy God. In an act of indescribable grace, God imputed to our account the righteousness of Christ. No court of law can justify. It may acquit or pardon, but only a righteous God can take someone guilty like me and justify me, treating me as if I have never sinned! We are "justified freely by His grace through the redemption that is in Christ Jesus" (Romans 3:24).

The final link in this chain is about the *worship* of our great God: "whom He justified, these He also glorified" (Romans 8:30). The verb tense in all of these links is amazing. It indicates an action in the past that has been completed. In other words, God speaks of our coming glorification as if it is already done. Justification means I have been saved from the *penalty* of sin by Jesus' death on the cross on my behalf. Sanctification means I am being saved from the *power* of sin right now. And glorification means one day I will be saved from the very *presence* of sin because I will be with my Lord and Savior in heaven.

God is watching over us, and He is working for our good. No wonder Paul asked, "If God be for us, who can be against us?"

Q & A : *"If God be for us, who can be against us?"* Since God is for us—stop at that fact and be amazed. The all-powerful, all-loving, always good, always wise God is on your side! Who can be against you then? Nothing and no one.

48 Do You Not Know That Your Body Is *the* Temple *of the* Holy Spirit Who Is *in* You?

—1 CORINTHIANS 6:19

This question comes in the context of the apostle Paul's admonition to "flee sexual immorality" (1 Corinthians 6:18). And Paul clearly stated the reason for this admonition: because "you are not your own. . . . You were bought at a price; therefore glorify God in your body" (vv. 19–20). Sandwiched between these two verses is the striking question, "Don't you know that your body is God's own temple?"

You've probably noticed: sex sells in modern America. It sells blue jeans, music, cars, computers, cameras, even mouthwash. Everyone is talking about sex today—everyone except for moms and dads in the home, and preachers and teachers in the church. So young people learn about sex from the hottest new entertainers of this day and the media—voices that too often fill their minds with immoral, if not utterly wrong, information. More than one generation in America has been raised with little to no moral absolutes, so relativism has taken root, influencing the thought processes of too many individuals away from God's truth. What was yesterday's shocking behavior is today's norm. What used to slither down the darkened back alleys now struts proudly down Main Street.

Two thousand years ago the apostle Paul confronted this very issue head-on when he wrote to a Corinthian culture as depraved and perverted as our own today. In the midst of all the decadence and perversion, Paul asked the Corinthians—and us: "Do you not know that your body is the temple of the Holy Spirit who is in you?"

AN ADMONITION

Notice the force and urgency of Paul's admonition "Flee sexual immorality" (1 Corinthians 6:18). Of course he was not exhorting us to flee sex. Within the marriage relationship, where it is intended, sex is pure and beautiful. When Paul said, "Flee!" he was addressing sexual immorality. The Greek word from which we get *immorality* is the same root from which the word *pornography* comes. Paul was commanding God's people to flee sexual encounters and acts that fall outside the biblical boundaries.

Paul admonished believers to flee, to run, to get out of there. While a slave in Egypt, Joseph did exactly that—he resisted Potiphar's wife's seductive advances. Joseph said no at the very onset and fled immediately. Like Joseph, we are to consciously, purposefully, and even perpetually run away from sexual immorality whenever we notice it lurking.

Some individuals, however, try to fight rather than flee. Overconfident, they think they can resist the temptation and handle the situation. To this Paul simply said, "Let him who thinks he stands take heed lest he falls" (10:12). I think it's quite significant that Paul didn't say, "Fight sexual immorality." He admonished us to "flee sexual immorality."

The reason we should run from every temptation to sexual immorality is because it can devastate three types of relationships—with others, with our own selves, and with God. In other words, sexual immorality affects our witness to others, our own sense of worth, and our worship of God. Sexual sins leave a mark on our soul and have an insidious way of mastering us. They can too easily define us and dominate us. So "flee sexual immorality" is the admonition to follow.

AN ADMISSION

Our bodies are temples of the Holy Spirit. In the New Testament, two Greek words translate into our English word *temple*. One is used to describe the entire temple complex in Jerusalem: the Temple Mount, the Court of the Gentiles, Solomon's Portico, the colonnades, and all the inner courts. The second word is used exclusively to describe that sacred space just beyond the veil in the Holy Place of the temple, the sacred space known as the Holy of Holies. It was there that God visited His people on the annual Day of Atonement. Significantly, when Paul wrote that your body is the temple of the Holy Spirit, he used this second word. He asserted that the believer's very body has become the Holy of Holies to God and the very dwelling place of His Spirit.

In the Old Testament, when God visited the Holy of Holies in His shekinah glory, He inhabited the space between the cherubim over the mercy seat of the ark. But today, in our dispensation of grace, He has chosen the bodies of His believers as His own sacred dwelling place. In the Old Testament, God had a temple for His people; since New Testament times He has His people as His temple. That means you and me!

Even people involved in illicit sexual sins would probably not think of committing those sins in a holy place; they wouldn't think of desecrating a church altar with their sin. So believers should recoil even more at the thought of committing such sin at all, for it is our very body that is God's temple, not some physical edifice. As Paul reminded the Corinthians, our bodies were "bought at a price" (1 Corinthians 6:20); our bodies are not our own, so we have absolutely no right to injure or defile what does not belong to us.

AN AMBITION

Finally, the apostle Paul set forth an appropriate ambition or purpose for our lives: "glorify God in your body and in your spirit, which are God's" (1 Corinthians 6:20). Our ambition in life is not to act according to our personal whims or desires, or to satisfy our personal pleasures. Our purpose in life is to glorify the Lord Jesus Christ.

Paul was very clear and straightforward: we ought to glorify God in all that we are and all that we do. This command is in the imperative mood, the very strongest language possible. Glorifying God is not an option for a believer. We are commanded to radiate the life and love of Christ with our whole being, and that includes our bodies.

God calls each of us to purity—to purity of mind, purity of motive, and purity of morals. Your body is God's temple, the place where His Holy Spirit has come to dwell. Therefore you are not really your own: you are purchased with the high price of Christ's blood. Therefore, glorify God with your body as well as your spirit. They belong to Him.

Q & A: "Do you not know that your body is the temple of the Holy Spirit who is in you?" If you didn't realize this before, you should now. You are so indescribably valuable to Jesus that He purchased your redemption with His own blood. Even before you were born, He knew you (Psalm 139:15). And now He has engraved your name on the palms of His hands (Isaiah 49:16). But that is not all. Today, right now, He has also chosen to make your body His own Holy Place, where He has taken up residency. No wonder Paul would later say, "Thanks be to God for His indescribable gift!" (2 Corinthians 9:15). No wonder we should glorify God in our bodies and in our spirits, which belong to Him!

49 How Shall We Escape If We Neglect So Great *a* Salvation?

—HEBREWS 2:3

*M*y wife, Susie, and I are fortunate enough to own a home. Recently, we had to replace some wooden eaves that were beginning to show signs of rot. The roof wasn't leaking yet, but we wanted to make sure it didn't. We call this preventive maintenance.

I own a car, and about every six months I take it to the dealership for a checkup and oil change.

I have a body, and every year in December I go in for a complete physical examination. I've learned that when something goes wrong with my home or my car or my body, it generally does so because of one thing: neglect.

If a little preventive maintenance is good for the physical matters of life, how much more imperative is it for the spiritual matters! The writer of Hebrews asks a penetrating and probing question: "How shall we escape if we neglect so great a salvation?" (2:3). The question is not addressed to those who flat-out reject the salvation claims of Christ, but to those who, perhaps with good intentions, simply procrastinate and neglect their spiritual health and well-being. It is closely akin to the question asked of us by our Lord in Mark 8:36: "For what will it profit a man if he shall gain the whole world, and lose his own soul?" How many times have we heard the worn out, but true, old adage, "The road to hell is paved with good intentions"?

A GREAT PROVISION

At issue here is salvation and whether we will spend eternity with God or apart from Him. God has provided forgiveness and salvation to whosoever will come to Him in repentance and faith. It is the free gift of eternal life. It is of little wonder then that the writer uses two qualifying words when speaking of this salvation. First, he describes it as "great." But there is more. He speaks of it as "so" great a salvation.

Our salvation is "so great" because of its *origin*: it is great because of the great love that made our salvation possible in the first place. Paul wrote that we who were dead in our sin have been saved "because of [God's] great love with which He loved us" (Ephesians 2:4). Our salvation is also great because God's great love not only prompted it, but He also provided it for us. God's great love is always accompanied by His great mercy: "For as the heavens are high above the earth, so great is His mercy toward those who fear Him" (Psalm 103:11).

Our salvation is not only great because of its origin but also because of its *outcome*. Our salvation is accompanied by great blessings of love, joy, peace, and so much more. Our gracious God has made a great provision for our "so great a salvation."

A GREAT PERIL

While salvation is a great provision, it comes with a great and potential peril. We will either escape or encounter that peril depending on our response to God's gift. "How shall we escape if we neglect so great a salvation?" There are three words that describe the response of every person toward the gospel: *reject*, *accept*, or *neglect*.

Some individuals have flat-out *rejected* the gospel message. They have consciously and deliberately refused the gift of eternal life. I have personally spoken to many people along life's pathway who have rejected the message of salvation and said no to the claims of Christ.

Other people have *accepted* the free gift of eternal life offered them through Jesus Christ our Lord. They have heard the gospel message, believed it, received it by faith, repented of their sins, and trusted in His finished work to save them. Though undeserving, I thank God each morning that I am counted among these.

Finally, some individuals see themselves in a sort of spiritual no-man's land. They have neither rejected the gospel, nor have they accepted it. They are among the vast throng who have *neglected* the divine offer of salvation; they have simply put off the decision for the present. They are deceived into thinking there will always be adequate time to name Jesus as their Savior and Lord before they die.

The writer of Hebrews warned that our hearts can become hardened (Hebrews 3:8). The apostle Paul added that those who continue to neglect Jesus' invitation to eternal life can become "past feeling" (Ephesians 4:19). The Greek word found here is the same from which we derive our English word *callus*. I have a callus on my hand that has become so hardened I can stick a pin into it and not even feel any pain. That skin is "past feeling." And this same kind of callus can appear on a human heart that continues to neglect the call of the gospel. Every time God calls us to decide and we postpone our decision, the callus on our heart gets a bit thicker. As He continues to call us unto Himself, and we continue to neglect the call, our hearts can become so hardened that, like the callus on my hand, there comes a time when we no longer can sense Him. We are "past feeling." When this happens, it doesn't mean He no longer is knocking on our hearts, but it does mean we will no longer be aware. That hardened heart is the great peril of neglect. No wonder the writer of Hebrews asked, "How shall we escape if we neglect so great a salvation?" (2:3).

Perhaps there is someone reading these words at this very moment who would never put off paying their bills or running their business or studying for class. Somehow, tragically, some think it is different with the spiritual matters of the soul. Hell is full of people who had good intentions of one day seriously considering and even accepting Jesus' invitation, but they never seemed to get around to making spiritual matters a priority.

God offers you and me salvation . . . And not just salvation, but great salvation . . . And not just great salvation, but *so great a salvation*! How shall we escape . . . if we neglect it?

Q & A: *"How shall we escape if we neglect so great a salvation?"* There is no escape from eternal separation from God if we neglect the salvation Jesus offers us. Only three roads lie before us. You can take the road less traveled and *accept* the gospel. You can take the road some travel and flat-out *reject* it. Or, tragically, you can continue on down the road and *neglect* the gospel to your own eternal peril. If so, what will it profit you, even if you gained the whole world, to lose your own soul in the end? Remember, not to decide is to decide! Call on God . . . right now. Say with Simon Peter, "Lord, save me." For "whoever calls on the name of the LORD shall be saved" (Romans 10:13).

50 What Does It Profit, My Brethren, If Someone Says He Has Faith *but* Does Not Have Works? Can Faith Save Him?

—JAMES 2:14

*T*hroughout Christian history, people have tried to pit Paul, with his emphasis on grace, against James, with his emphasis on works. The apparent conflict has been presented like the main event of a heavyweight prizefight: "In this corner, wearing the grace trunks, is the apostle Paul, born in Tarsus, educated by the renowned Gamaliel, and the undisputed brilliant mind of this new movement called Christianity! He says, 'By grace you have been saved through faith, and that not of yourselves; it is the gift of God' (Ephesians 2:8). And in the other corner, wearing the works trunks is James, the son of Joseph and Mary from Nazareth, converted after the resurrection of Jesus, and known as the respected leader of the Jerusalem church! He teaches, 'Faith without works is dead' (James 2:26)." In some Christian circles, the prizefight between faith and works continues two thousand years later.

The ongoing debate over the nature of salvation tends to gravitate toward two extremes. One school of thought is often referred to as "easy believism." This overemphasis on faith and underemphasis on fruit, or works, leads some to say that people can pray a simple "sinner's prayer" when they are children, live the rest of their days with no desire whatsoever for spiritual things, and still be saved from the consequences of their sin and God's wrath to come. The other extreme overemphasizes works and underemphasizes faith. This ideology teaches that it is faith plus something else (like baptism or some other kind of human effort) that saves. Still other Christians believe God has some type of huge scale, and they hope that when the final bell rings, their good works will outweigh their bad, and all will end well.

Let's get inside the ring with Paul and James, between grace and works, and see if we can determine the winner.

ROUND ONE: PAUL ON THE OFFENSE

Paul begins with a left jab: he says, "For by grace you have been saved" (Ephesians 2:8). He plunges right into the fight insisting that salvation is *God's work*, that salvation is "by grace." God's gift of salvation is not in response to any of our human efforts. It originates with Him, not with man. Our salvation is by grace, a word that can be defined as "getting what we don't deserve." Again, Paul taught that grace is "the gift of God" (v. 8), a blessing freely given by the Father, a blessing that can never be earned.

As quick as a flash Paul strikes again with a right cross to the chin when he explains that salvation is *God's work in God's way*. Paul insists that salvation comes "through faith, and that not of yourselves" (v. 8). Salvation is God's work, and it must be accomplished in God's way, which is through faith in Jesus Christ. Even as I type these words, I find myself wanting to shout, *"By faith! Not of yourselves! Not of works! The gift of God!"*

Do you realize that there are only two religions in the whole world? They are true religion and false religion. True religion originates in Jesus Christ, who said, "I am the way, the truth, and the life. No one comes to the Father except through Me" (John 14:6).

Paul, sensing an opportunity, now delivers an uppercut: "Salvation is *God's work in God's way according to God's will.*" Paul continues, "For we are [God's] workmanship, created in Christ Jesus for good works, which God prepared beforehand that we should walk in them" (Ephesians 2:10). God created each one of us unique, His own one-of-a-kind work of art; no one else on the planet has DNA like yours. And that is not all: God prepared us "beforehand," back in the eternal recesses of time. So Paul makes a strong case for grace. James seems to be on the ropes.

ROUND TWO: JAMES COUNTERS

James stands his ground. He is now toe-to-toe with Paul. He counters, "A faith without fruit is a *false faith.*" More specifically, James asks, "What good is it if you say you have faith and have not works? Can this kind of faith save you?" (James 2:14, paraphrased).

With lightning speed he keeps coming: "Faith without fruit is not only false faith; it is also *futile faith.*" Then James issues this challenge: "You say you have faith. Show me! Even the demons believe and tremble" (vv. 18–19, paraphrased).

James stands his ground now. He continues, "A faith without fruit is also a *fatal faith*." He explains this important point: "Just as the body without the spirit is dead, so faith without works is DOA, dead on arrival" (vv. 20–26, paraphrased).

THE FINAL BELL

When the bell rings, both Paul and James are still standing. In fact, they are actually hugging each other. Then, at the same moment, they grab the other's arm and lift it high in victory. They both win! How? Because in the final analysis, these two men of God are saying the same thing. The judges determine that Paul is saying what James is saying: "We are [God's] workmanship, created in Christ Jesus *for good works*!" (Ephesians 2:10, emphasis added). And James is saying what Paul is saying: "Of [God's] own will He brought us forth [chose us] by the word of truth" (James 1:18). The teachings of these men of God complement each other; they are not contradictory.

Paul was primarily writing to the Judaizers, those people of the Jewish faith who had infiltrated the early church with their false teaching that people had to add to faith works that were in line with ancient Jewish law in order to be saved. In response, Paul emphasized the primacy of faith: salvation is wholly by grace and through faith alone. James, on the other hand, was writing primarily to people who went to the far extreme of grace and insisted that they could live any way they wanted as long as they "believed." Thus James's emphasis was on what our Lord called the fruit of our faith. What evidence of your faith do others see in your life?

So faith *and* works walk out of the ring arm in arm. That is as it should be, because this fight about the Christian life is not about faith *and* works but about a faith *that* works. Thus works are never a requirement for our salvation; works are the result of our salvation. Yes, it is faith alone that saves, but faith that saves is never alone! Faith that saves is never isolated from works.

Q & A: *"What does it profit, my brethren, if someone says he has faith but does not have works? Can faith save him?"* The question is not whether faith can save us or not, but whether a faith that never produces what our Lord called the "fruit of the Spirit" (Ephesians 5:9) can save us. The real issue is not about faith *and* works, but a faith *that* works!

51 WHAT IS YOUR LIFE?

—JAMES 4:14

*T*hese four simple words ask a very profound question: "What is your life?" While mystery shrouds what took place before the cradle and what will take place after the grave, the biggest mystery of all is life itself—the time between the cradle and the grave when we are encased in human flesh. How did we get here? Why are we here? What are we to be doing here? Where are we headed? Is this all there is? The question of our chapter—"What is your life?"—prompts many such questions.

Today's culture puts enormous pressure on us to focus most of our attention on the here and now. For too many of us, biblical views of life and death are overshadowed, if not totally forgotten. We too easily live as though this life is all there is and all that matters. We seek to camouflage the aging process so as to pretend we are avoiding it. We cram any thoughts of death or the afterlife into the far recesses of our minds. We live as if we have a ninety-nine-year lease on our bodies with an option to renew. And all of this is ironic in light of the fact that the greatest certainty life holds for us is our upcoming appointment with death. That reality makes "What is your life?" an important question for everyone to answer.

LIFE HAS ITS UNCERTAINTIES

What is your life? Secular scientists and philosophers cannot satisfactorily answer this question. Christians, on the other hand, understand that death is not an end but a means to an end: when believers die, they don't leave home; they go home.

This perspective is invaluable as we face the mystery of life and its uncertainties. We celebrate our birthday and number our years, but the psalmist says to number our days: "Teach us to number our days, that we may gain a heart of wisdom" (Psalm 90:12).

The question James not only asked but also answered in the same verse may help us number our days. Consider this description of life: "It is even a vapor that appears for a little time and then vanishes away" (James 4:14). A vapor is here one moment and gone the next. Like steam coming out of a tea kettle on the stove, our life on this planet appears for a short while and then vanishes. This calls to mind the famous line in Shakespeare's *Macbeth*: "Out, out, brief candle! Life is but a walking shadow, a poor player that struts and frets his hours upon the stage, and then is heard no more." Life is brief and filled with uncertainties: we can't know what will happen next in our life or in the lives of those we love.

LIFE HAS ITS CERTAINTIES

Life is only a vapor that quickly fades. We may frantically look to miracle drugs to add a few more months to life. Some even rush to cryonics and seek to freeze their bodies after death in hopes that future medical science will find ways to cure their disease and bring them back to life. Still, life's greatest certainty is our appointment with death. The Bible says, "It is appointed for men to die once, but after this the judgment" (Hebrews 9:27).

Peter Marshall, former pastor and chaplain of the United States Senate (1902–1949) once told an Arabic fable that illustrates this certainty. A merchant in Baghdad sent his servant to the market. When he returned, the servant was pale and trembling. Clearly upset, he said to his master, "Down in the marketplace I was jostled by a woman in the crowd. When I turned around, I saw that it was Death that jostled me. She looked at me and made a threatening gesture. Please, lend me a horse that I may hasten to Samarra and hide there so Death will not find me."

The merchant gave him a horse, and the servant galloped away in haste. Later the merchant went to the marketplace and saw Death standing in the crowd. He went over to her and asked, "Why did you frighten my servant this morning? Why did you make a threatening gesture?"

Death replied, "That was not a threatening gesture. I was only startled and surprised to see him in Baghdad, for I have an appointment with him tonight in Samarra!"*

Each of us has our own appointment in Samarra, but if we have put our faith and trust in Christ, this appointment should not cause fear but rejoicing. Our hope in Christ enables us to sing, "Because He lives, I can face tomorrow." We are never really ready to live until we are ready to die.

When we acknowledge that Jesus died on the cross as payment for our sins, we can look forward to eternity with Him, an eternity where "there shall be no more death, nor sorrow, nor crying. There shall be no more pain" (Revelation 21:4). Trusting Him and knowing Him in the free pardoning of sin takes away the fear of death, and the absence of that fear enables us to live life to the fullest with great joy and hope and peace.

Life is only a vapor. In the context of eternity, we are on this small planet in this vast universe for a short period of time. Ultimately, it doesn't matter who we know, how high we may have climbed a social or business ladder, or how many goods we have accumulated. All that matters in this life and in the next is our response to the Lord Jesus Christ.

Q & A: *"What is your life?"* One day someone will look at your tombstone and note the year of your birth or the year of your death. But what matters most will be hidden in the dash between those years, specifically, what your response to Jesus was when you walked this earth. After all, the quality of one's life is never determined by the number of years. Some live a life long in years but not especially rich. Others live a full, rich, and significant life in only a few years. Make sure the years represented by your dash are characterized by your preparation for the next life, by your focus on your relationship with Jesus. After all, as James wrote, "What is your life? It is even a vapor that appears for a little time and then vanishes away" (James 4:14). Trust in Christ so that when your appointed time comes, you have the rock-solid assurance that, rather than leaving home, you are actually going home.

* *John Doe, Disciple* by Peter Marshall, copyright © 1963 by McGraw-Hill Book Company, Inc., first edition, pp 219–220.

52   Is Anyone Among You Sick?

*J*ames wrote to believers who had fled Jerusalem under great persecution, and his letter is amazingly relevant to modern Christianity on several points. He, for instance, called on the church to be in touch with the hurting world that is all around us. We live in the midst of a world of hurts. Hearts are hurting. Families are hurting. Tragically, when people today hear the word *church*, they too often think of a musty-smelling, irrelevant institution out of touch with real human need. Have we looked around us lately? People are not simply sick physically but mentally, emotionally, and spiritually sick. Thus, we find ourselves asking an extremely pertinent question for our own culture: "Is anyone among you sick?"

Perhaps no other ministry of the New Testament church has seen as much perversion as the church's healing ministry. While many involved may have wonderful intentions and pure hearts, some healing ministries have too often been a vehicle for a few to build their own personal financial kingdoms by offering false hopes of healing to any and all who come their way. Here in James 5, we find the only directive in Scripture concerning praying for those who are sick.

Contextually James described a local church ministry at a member's bedside. After all, who most needs healing? Is it the person who can get up, get dressed, drive to the city auditorium, listen to a flashy and fancy preacher, and then stand in a "healing line" for an extended period of time? Or is the one who cannot get out of bed in greater need of the Great Physician's healing touch?

THE PROBE

"Is anyone among you sick?" The key to understanding this question is the word *sick*. James chose a word in Greek that means "without strength" or "to be weak." Erroneously, we often assume that only physical sickness is involved. However, the word can include those who are weak in body, in soul, or in spirit. Note the next verse where James said, "The prayer of faith will save the sick" (v. 15). Here the word *sick* is a different word meaning "to grow weary."

James was writing to those who had "grown weary" in the struggles of life, those "scattered abroad" (James 1:1) in the great dispersion. They had been forced to flee their homes and their jobs. Tempted to give out and give up, they were weary and weak. While these verses can certainly be applied to people who are physically sick, James was primarily writing to those about to crack mentally under the pressures of life.

THE PROPOSAL

James's proposal is for those who are weak and weary to "call for the elders of the church" (James 5:14). Those who are sick spiritually and emotionally often need someone upon whom they can lean and from whom they can draw strength. But the initiative is to be taken by those who are sick themselves. Anyone who has ever served as a pastor or elder has more than once heard, "No one ever came to visit me when I was sick." But in James 5, the onus is on the one who is sick to take the initiative in calling for the elders. In response to this initiative, the elders are then instructed to perform their ministry of encouragement, to—as Paul exhorted— "comfort the fainthearted, uphold the weak, be patient with all" (1 Thessalonians 5:14).

THE PROCEDURE

When a sick person calls for the elders, they are to "pray over him, anointing him with oil in the name of the Lord" (James 5:14). In the Greek language in which James wrote, there are two distinct words translated into our English word *anoint*. One refers to an outward anointing; literally, a "rubbing down with oil." The word is found in the story of the good Samaritan who bandaged the wounded man, "pouring" oil and wine into the wounds to fight infection and soothe the hurt. The other Greek word translated into English as *anoint* has to do with a ceremonial anointing used in a sacred and symbolic sense. Jesus, for example, explained that the Spirit "anointed" Him to preach the gospel (Luke 4:18).

Today, when the sick are anointed with oil and prayed for, the anointing is usually done in the symbolic sense. A drop or two of oil is placed on the finger and touched on the forehead, often in the sign of a cross. While there is nothing wrong in doing this, it is not at all the procedure that James described. He used the word that instructs us to do what the good Samaritan did: rub the wounded and the sick with oil. Pour wine into his wounds. In other words, use the best medicine known to man. The church should support the efforts of those in the medical community to bring healing, and those in the medical world should support the healing efforts in the church by recognizing the importance of the prayer of faith.

THE PRAYER

This prayer at the bedside of the sick must be "the prayer of faith" (James 5:15). Earlier in his letter, James indicated that when we pray, we must believe, asking "in faith with no doubting, for he who doubts is like a wave of the sea driven and tossed by the wind" (1:6).

Furthermore, the prayer of faith must always be offered according to God's Word and His will. When my wife and I were raising our daughters, we did not always give them everything for which they asked. Many times we knew what was best for them when they didn't. Quite honestly, looking back over my life, I am extremely grateful God didn't give me everything for which I asked of Him. At times, my own personal preferences or prejudices clouded my thinking and took precedence over His will for my life. I have asked Him time and again for certain things I now see He had no intention of giving because He had something far better in mind. It is appealing to hear preachers say, "You can have anything you ask." But that request is not biblical. The prayer of faith *must* be grounded in the Word of God, or it is not the prayer of faith. After all, in the words of Paul, "faith comes by hearing, and hearing by the word of God" (Romans 10:17).

THE PROVISION

"The prayer of faith will save the sick, and the Lord will raise him up" (James 5:15). This verse is not a carte blanche for healing. It is wrapped in the mystery of God's will and way. After all, Paul once left Trophimus while he was sick at Miletus instead of healing him (2 Timothy 4:20). Paul allowed Epaphroditus to become ill and almost die (Philippians 2:25–30). Paul even asked the Lord repeatedly to remove his own "thorn in the flesh," only to discover that God's grace was all-sufficient (2 Corinthians 12:7, 9). And once Paul instructed Timothy to drink a little wine for his "frequent infirmities" (1 Timothy 5:23).

Physical healing is a mystery wrapped up in the counsel of God's own will. Some say all can be healed, yet God didn't heal Paul when he asked. Others say that illness is the result of sin, yet some of God's greatest saints have known the greatest suffering. Others say healing has to do with your attitude, yet no one had a more pitiful attitude than Naaman who was healed of leprosy (2 Kings 5:11–14).

All healing is divine. Medicine alone doesn't heal. Doctors alone do not heal. Proper diet alone doesn't heal. Exercise alone doesn't heal. God heals! God's own name is Jehovah Rapha . . . the God who heals! And we can trust the One who always has our very best interest at heart.

Q & A: *"Is anyone among you sick?"* Perhaps, even as you read these words, you are in pain or have heard the doctor say, "You have cancer." Remember, God never slumbers nor sleeps (Psalm 121:4). He is awake and aware. Call some praying friends, lean on them and their prayers, believe that our God can still make the impossible possible, and surrender yourself into the loving hands of Jesus and His perfect will for your life.

Epilogue

I am often asked why I chose these fifty-two particular questions from the more than three thousand questions recorded in Scripture. My goal in these pages was to address the broadest spectrum of topics possible. This necessitated my leaving out some of my own favorite Scripture questions. (That fact just may call for a *Jesus Code II* with fifty-two more Scripture questions every believer should be able to answer— as well as a *Joshua Code II* with fifty-two more Scripture verses every believer should know!)

One such question—omitted because so many that were included dealt with the same subject—was that of Pontius Pilate, the Roman governor of Judea, who asked, "What shall I do with Jesus who is called Christ?" (Matthew 27:22). This is the question each of us must confront. You will either accept Him . . . or reject Him. You will either say yes to Him . . . or no to Him. Not to decide on this issue . . . is to decide.

It may be that, while you were journeying through these pages, God's Spirit has been nudging you to put your faith and trust in Christ for the forgiveness of your sin and the gift of eternal life. Heaven is God's personal and free gift to you: it cannot be earned, nor will you ever deserve it. We are all sinners who have fallen short of God's perfect standard for our lives. He is a God of love and does not want to punish us for our sins, but He is also a God of justice and therefore must punish sin.

This is where Jesus stepped in. He is the holy and sinless God-man who came to take your sins in His own body and die on the cross as punishment for your sins. However, just knowing this fact is not enough. You must transfer your trust from yourself and your own human efforts to Christ alone and put your faith in Him for your own personal salvation.

Jesus said, "Behold, I stand at the door and knock. If anyone hears My voice and opens the door, I will come in to him" (Revelation 3:20). If you would like to receive this free gift of eternal life, you can call on Jesus right now . . . this very moment. He promised that "whoever calls on the name of the LORD shall be saved" (Romans 10:13). The following is a suggested prayer:

Dear Lord Jesus,

I know I have sinned; I know I don't deserve eternal life in and of myself. Please forgive me for my sin— and thank You for taking on my sin in Your body and dying on the cross on my behalf. I trust in You as the only One who saves me from eternal separation from a Holy God. Come into my life right now. I accept Your free and gracious offer of forgiveness, abundant life, and eternal life. Thank You for coming into my life as my Savior and my Lord.

A prayer cannot save you, but Jesus can save you—and He will. If this prayer reflects the desire of your heart, you can claim the promise Jesus made to those who believe in Him: "Most assuredly . . . he who believes in Me has everlasting life" (John 6:47).

You can now join millions of Christ's followers in answering Pilate's question, "What shall I do with Jesus who is called Christ?" by confidently affirming, "I will believe Jesus is the one and only Savior, and I will put my trust in Him . . . for now and for eternity."

Mission:Dignity

*A*ll of the author's royalties and any proceeds from *The Jesus Code* and *The Joshua Code* go to the support of Mission:Dignity, a ministry of the Dallas-based GuideStone Financial Resources that enables thousands of retired ministers (and, in most cases, their widows) who are living near the poverty level to live out their days with dignity and security. Many of them spent their pastoral ministry in small churches that were unable to provide adequately for their retirement. They also lived in church-owned parsonages and, upon their vocational retirement, had to vacate them as well. Mission:Dignity is a way of letting these good and godly servants know they are not forgotten and will be cared for in their declining years.

All of the expenses of this ministry are paid out of an endowment that has been raised for such, so that everyone who gives to Mission:Dignity can be assured that every cent of their gift goes to one of these precious saints in need.

For additional information regarding this ministry, please go to www.guidestone.org and click on the Mission:Dignity icon, or call toll-free at 1-888-98-GUIDE (1-888-984-8433).

TRANSFORM YOUR HEART WITH

God's Word

The Joshua Code is designed to walk you through a year-long journey of meditating on one verse a week in order to recall and recite Scripture at will. Topics include temptation, understanding salvation, prayer, grace, vision, integrity, and more.

The Jesus Code takes you on a journey with one critical question each week to study and meditate on until the answer is firmly fixed in your mind and heart. Those answers will show God's will for your life, and they will help you feel confident as you share your faith with others.

The James Code challenges readers to give feet to their faith with applicable truth from the book of James emphasizing that an effective Christian life is not about faith and works, but is about faith that works.

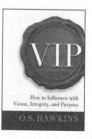

VIP takes readers through what it takes to create a life of Vision, Influence, and Purpose. Through inspirational stories, biblical examples, and charged challenges toward greatness, *VIP* illuminates a path for you to uncover what it is going to take for you to become a VIP, a Very Influential Person.

100% of the author's royalties and proceeds goes to support Mission:Dignity—a ministry providing support for impoverished retired pastors and missionaries.

Available at bookstores everywhere!

THOMAS NELSON
Since 1798

OTHER BOOKS *by* O. S. HAWKINS

When Revival Comes
(with Jack R. Taylor)

After Revival Comes

Clues to a Successful Life

Where Angels Fear to Tread

*Tracing the Rainbow
Through the Rain*

Revive Us Again

Unmasked!

*Jonah: Meeting the God of
the Second Chance*

In Sheep's Clothing

*Tearing Down Walls and
Building Bridges*

*Moral Earthquakes and
Secret Faults*

*Rebuilding: It's Never Too Late
for a New Beginning*

*Money Talks: But What Is
It Really Saying?*

*Shields of Brass or
Shields of Gold?*

Good News for Great Days

Drawing the Net

Culture Shock

High Calling, High Anxiety

The Question for Our Time

The Art of Connecting

GuideStones: Ancient Landmarks

The Pastor's Primer

More Good News for Great Days

Getting Down to Brass Tacks

Antology

*The Pastor's Guide to
Leading and Living*

*The Joshua Code: 52
Scripture Verses Every
Believer Should Know*

About *the* Author

*F*or more than twenty-five years, O. S. Hawkins served pastorates including the First Baptist Church in Fort Lauderdale, Florida, and the First Baptist Church in Dallas, Texas. A native of Fort Worth, he has three earned degrees (BBA, MDiv, and DMin) and several honorary degrees. He is president of GuideStone Financial Resources, which serves 200,000 pastors, church staff members, missionaries, doctors, nurses, university professors, and other workers in various Christian organizations with their retirement and benefit service needs. He is the author of more than twenty-five books, including the bestselling *The Joshua Code*, and preaches regularly at Bible conferences, evangelism conferences, and churches across the nation. He and his wife, Susie, have two married daughters and six grandchildren.

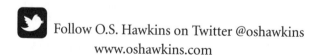

Follow O.S. Hawkins on Twitter @oshawkins
www.oshawkins.com

East of the Sun, West of the Moon

Retold by Susanna Davidson
Illustrated by Petra Brown

Reading consultant: Alison Kelly
Roehampton University

Contents

Chapter 1

The white bear

Far away to the north, where
the land is covered in thick, dark
forests and the wind blows bitterly
cold, there lived a poor family.

3

Late one afternoon, they sat
huddled around the hearth.
The firelight flickered over the
children's faces.

The boys were handsome, the
girls pretty – but the youngest,
Asta, was the most beautiful of all.

4

As dusk began to close in around the cottage, there came a knock at the door. "Who's there?" called the father. But there was no answer.

So the father rose and opened the
door, letting in a rush of icy air.
Before him stood a towering
white bear.

"I have watched your family
all summer," said the bear, in a
rumbling voice. "And I am ready to
make you an offer."

"If you give me your youngest daughter," he went on, "I can make you as rich as you are now poor."

"I'll not give you my daughter," said the father, blocking the way, "however poor we may be."

7

But Asta looked into the sad,
black eyes of the great white bear,
and made up her mind.

"We barely have enough food to
eat," she said. "And our clothes are
turning to rags. How will we survive
the winter? I will go with the bear."

So saying, she stood up, collected
a small bundle of belongings and
walked steadily to the door.

"Don't go!" cried her mother.

"The bear must be under a spell,"
she whispered in her daughter's ear.

"Don't worry, Mother," said Asta,
"I am not afraid."

9

Asta climbed on
the bear's back.
"Keep a tight
hold of my fur,"
he told her.

Then, before anyone could
stop him, he bounded away
into the night.

10

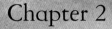

Chapter 2

Inside the mountain

While the moon was still high in
the sky, Asta and the bear arrived
at a craggy black mountain.

11

The bear raised his huge paw
and knocked on the mountainside.
A door creaked open...

Inside, was a glittering castle,
carved from stone.

12

The white bear handed Asta a
golden bell. "Ring this if you need
anything," he said.

No sooner had Asta taken the
bell, than she found herself alone in
a grand bedroom. She lay down on
the bed, but couldn't sleep.

13

Clouds passed over the moon,
sinking the castle into darkness.
Footsteps echoed down the corridor.
Asta peered out from her room,
and saw a man in the shadows.

He dragged behind him
a white bear skin, which
gleamed in the moonlight.

14

Each night after that, Asta
watched the man until he
disappeared into one of the rooms.
"Is that the bear, changed into a
man?" she wondered.

She longed to see his face.

The days rolled on. Asta had
everything she could ask for. And,
each evening, the bear would come
and sit by her side. She would
stroke his soft fur and sing to him.

The bear would rest his head on
her lap, with a glimmer of hope in
his dark eyes.

16

But Asta felt lonely in the castle,
with the bear who rarely spoke.
All day she would sit and wonder
about the man who walked in
the shadows.

The white bear watched the
roses fade from her cheeks. "What
is it?" he asked one day. "What
do you want?"

"I want to go home," Asta replied, "just for a day, to see my family again."

"That can be arranged," said the white bear. "If you will only promise me not to talk to your mother alone."

The next day, they set out on the long journey, with Asta astride the white bear's back.

At last they came to a large farmhouse. "This is where your family lives now," said the white bear.

"I will leave you for a night and a day. But don't forget what I said, or you will do much harm to us both."

I promise.

Asta was filled with happiness to see her family again. But before she left, her mother managed to get her alone.

Asta soon told her about the man who paced the corridors at night – and how she'd never seen his face.

"You might be living with a troll!" her mother said. "You must take a candle. Hide it in your clothes and light it when he's asleep."

That night, Asta kindled her
light, then followed the man to his
room. She held it above his sleeping
form, and saw the handsomest
prince of her dreams.

Unable to resist, she bent down
and kissed his cheek. As she did
so, three hot drops of wax fell
upon his shirt.

The prince woke with a start.
"What have you done?" he cried.
"I've been bewitched by the troll
queen, so I'm a bear by day and a
man by night."

"I was to be set free if I could find a
girl who would love me for a year...
without seeing my human face."

23

"Now I must go to the
castle that lies east of the
sun and west of the moon.
And there I must marry
the troll queen."

"Can't I go with you?"
Asta begged.
"No," answered the prince.

24

"The troll queen has me under a powerful spell. I *must* go to her."

"Then I'll follow you there," vowed Asta.

"You can try," said the prince sadly, "but you'll never find me."

Chapter 3

Golden gifts

When Asta awoke the next
morning, both the prince and
the castle had gone.

She was lying in a forest clearing, with nothing but the clothes she came in. "I'll head north," Asta decided, "because that is where the trolls dwell."

Asta walked for many days and many nights, until her feet were sore and her legs were weary.

27

She thought of her last journey on the white bear's back – the feel of his thick, soft fur and the speed at which he bounded along.

"I'll never find him," she wept.

"You shouldn't give up so easily," croaked a voice. Asta looked up to see an old woman standing beside a horse.

"Can you help me?" Asta asked, eagerly. "I'm looking for my prince. He's in the castle that lies east of the sun and west of the moon."

"Aha!" said the old woman. "So you're the girl. I've heard tales of you and your search."

I will help you.

"I'll give you my horse and three golden gifts," she went on, handing Asta a comb, an apple and a pear.

"Where shall I go?" asked Asta. "To find the castle, ride until you meet the East Wind," the old woman said. "That is all I know."

Asta climbed on the horse's back and the old woman whispered in its ear. A moment later, they were off.

"Thank you!" called Asta, as her voice was whipped away by the wind.

Chapter 4

The four winds

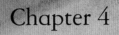

The horse's hooves pounded over the ground. Faster and faster he flew and Asta clung to his mane.

33

On a cliff top overlooking a
rolling sea, the horse finally came
to a stop. All around them, the
East Wind blew in gentle gusts.

"Can you tell me the way to the
castle that lies east of the sun and
west of the moon?" Asta asked.

34

"I have never blown that far," the East Wind replied. "But I will take you to my brother, the West Wind. He may know the way, for he is much stronger than I."

Asta climbed on the East Wind's back and they roared away over the waves, to the land where the West Wind lived.

"Brother," called the East Wind, "do you know the way to the castle that lies east of the sun and west of the moon?"

"No," said the West Wind. "I have never blown that far. But I will take the girl to the South Wind, for he is much stronger than either of us and has roamed far and wide."

So they rode to the land where
the South Wind lived.

"Only the North Wind knows
the way to the castle," said the
South Wind, "for he is the oldest
and strongest of us all. I will carry
you there."

When they came near the North
Wind, Asta felt his presence in the
frantic, icy blasts of air.

"What do you want?" he roared.

"I carry the one who seeks
the prince, in the castle east of
the sun and west of the moon,"
the South Wind replied.

38

"I know it," said the North Wind. "I blew there once, but I was so tired that for many days after, I could not blow at all."

"If you are not afraid to go with me," the North Wind went on, "I will take you there."

39

Asta thought of her
prince with his sad,
black eyes. "I am not
afraid," she said.

Then the North Wind puffed
himself up, until he was so big and
strong he was frightful to see.

40

Asta climbed on his back and
together they flew through the air,
as if they would not stop until they
reached the end of the world.

Below them, storms
raged over the oceans and
ships were tossed like toys on
the roaring waves.

41

At last they had gone so far that
even the North Wind felt tired.
He sank lower and lower,
until the waves dashed
against Asta's feet.

"Nearly... there..." puffed the
North Wind, and with a final gust,
he blew her onto an icy shore.

42

Above her, east of the
sun and west of the
moon, rose the troll
queen's castle.

Exhausted, Asta crawled into a
cave beneath the crags, and slept.

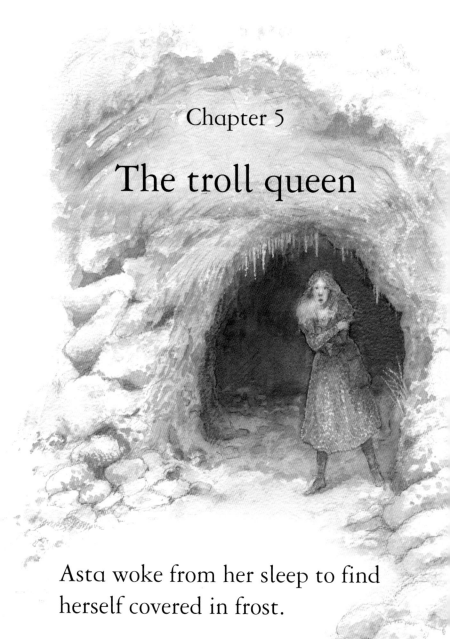

Chapter 5

The troll queen

Asta woke from her sleep to find
herself covered in frost.

44

With stiff limbs, she climbed
the crags to the castle door. From
behind a rock, she watched the
trolls lumbering in and out.

They carried buckets and mops,
rolls of red carpet and yards of
white silk.

"They're preparing for the wedding!" Asta gasped, and she slipped inside the castle to search for her prince.

The castle was filled with trolls... but her prince was nowhere to be seen.

Finally, she came to a grand
room lit by candlelight. There, on
a great stone throne, sat the troll
queen herself.

She had string-like hair which
she combed with long, yellow nails,
and a nose that drooped down to
her lap.

47

"What do you want?"
she asked, in a voice
like grinding stones.
"I've come to
see the prince,"
Asta replied.

The troll queen beckoned Asta
closer. "First you must give me
something in return," she said.

Asta looked down at her tattered clothes, then remembered the old woman's gifts. "I could give you this golden comb?" she said.

The troll queen grabbed it from her with a claw-like hand. "You may see the prince tonight," she snapped. "He's in the room at the top of the tallest tower."

That night, Asta rushed to the prince's room, and there she found him, fast asleep. She shook him and called to him but nothing would wake him.

In the morning, the troll queen returned. "Now get out of my castle!" she cried.

Asta spent the day in her cave. As evening drew in, she stood beneath the troll queen's window, playing with her golden apple.

"Give it to me!" the troll queen called from her window. "What will you give me in return?" asked Asta.

51

"You may visit the prince tonight," the troll queen replied.

But again there was no waking him. And, as soon as morning came, she was dragged from the castle by the troll queen's guards.

With one last gift to use, Asta stood beneath the troll queen's window once more. Her golden pear glinted in the pale light of the northern sun.

"You may see the prince tonight," gloated the troll queen, "in return for that shining pear."

53

"But it'll be the last time," she added, "for tomorrow we marry and then he'll be *mine*."

That night, like the others, the prince slept like one enchanted. Then it came to Asta how she might break the spell.

Hidden within the folds of her clothes, was the candle her mother had given her so long ago. She lit it and watched three drops of hot wax fall onto the sleeping prince...

With a start, he woke.

Chapter 6

The spell breaks

"You've come just in time," the prince cried. "I was to marry the troll queen tomorrow night, but you've found me before the year is out."

Then, from the stone turret, came
the sound of heavy feet.

"Hurry! We must flee,"
urged Asta. "The troll
queen is coming."

As she spoke, the first light of
dawn pricked the night sky.

57

"I am still a bear for
one more day," roared
the prince.

Turning, Asta saw he was a
white bear once more.
"Climb on my back," he said.

As the troll queen opened the
bedroom door, the bear charged
past her down the turret stairs.

"Come back!" she cried.
"Never," snarled the bear.
"Stop them," the troll queen
ordered her guards.

59

But the trolls were no match for the giant bear. With one swipe from his paw he scattered them like leaves, then burst through the castle door.

Together, Asta and the bear galloped to the icy shore. There, a boat bobbed on the water. In one bound, the bear leaped aboard.

"I thought you would need help escaping," said the North Wind. "All this time I have been resting. Now I will take you home."

For months, they journeyed south, the North Wind blowing the boat as gently as he could.

"I have lost my riches," the prince told Asta. "All my treasure is trapped in the troll queen's castle."

"She can keep it!" laughed Asta. "I know of a beautiful farmhouse where we can live..."

When at last they stepped off
the boat, Asta turned to the North
Wind and asked, "Why did you
and your brother winds help me?"

"Your story was foretold to us,"
the North Wind replied. "For you
are the girl who went to the ends of
the earth for love."